LANGUAGE WITHIN LANGUAGE

By

Maria Brusco Osso

TRUE PERSPECTIVE PUBLISHING HOUSE

LANGUAGE WITHIN LANGUAGE

www.trueperspectivepublishinghouse.com

Dedication:

Love is a word that countless civilizations have tried to define – all without success.

And that's because love is not a word – Love is an action. You see – words are easy.

When you want to know who or what you "love" – just take a look at what you are willing to sacrifice – your time, your energy, your money, and sometimes even your dreams and personal wishes.

When you boil it all down – Love is a Sacrifice.

God, our Father, told us that clearly in His Word over 2000 years ago. "For God so loved the world, that He gave His only begotten Son"…

Love GIVES to others what we hold dear.

Love Sacrifices

Love puts others first.

Gloria Veltri (1963-2016).

Acknowledgements:

I would like to thank Marissa Suriano, licensed mental health counselor for the research sample and administration of the study tool. Additionally, gratitude is extended to my daughter, Elisa Ilardi for her editing skills and recommendations.

TABLE OF CONTENTS:

INTRODUCTION

The present generation is said to be unlike those of previous ones, having been described as "discontinuously different." Discontinuously different describes a generation whose cultural environment is considerably diverse than those experienced in former generations. The cultural climate is so different that when it comes to the things of faith, the current generational response is, "Wait, I don't understand. You lost me" (Kinnaman).

David Kinnaman, head of the Barna Research Group and author of the book entitled, *You Lost Me, Why Young Christians Are Leaving Church and Rethinking Faith,* explains, "The current spiritual narrative... [as] akin to the difficulties of immigrant cultures have between generations. The first generation speaks only the language of the country of origin. The second generation is fluent in both languages. The third generation speaks the new language and has little esteem for the cultural traditions that have been lost in translation" (56). The latest Barna Research involving the present generation supports a potential disagreement in language. The language spoken to this generation has not changed but the meaning of the words have as evidenced by the inability to understand. Therefore, the contention of this book is that although the language spoken by many generations may have been adopted, the meaning of the words may have not. There is a language within the language.

The consequences of the phenomenon are extraordinary when placed in the light of God's commandment to "Train up a child in the way he should go; even when he is old he will not depart" (Proverbs 22:6). Paul reiterates, "But as for you, teach what accords with sound doctrine" (Titus 2:1). In his letter to the Colossians, Paul writes, "For the sake of his body, that is, his church of which I became a *minister* according to the stewardship from God that was given to me for you, to make the *word* of God *fully known*, the mystery hidden for ages and generations but now revealed to his saints" (1:24-25, my emphasis). The Greek word for minister is diakonos which refers to one who serves (Mounce). Paul is addressing the church of Colossae, to make known that he is entrusted as the servant of God, to teach the words of his Master. The purpose is to reveal God's redemptive plan for man through the Messiah Jesus. Jesus rescued man from death brought on by the original sin and offers the gift of everlasting life to all who believe in Him.

The ones who teach the words of God are called ministers. Minister, according to Scripture means "one who is in voluntary attendance upon another person. Joshua was the minister of Moses (Exodus 24:13) and Elisha was the minister of Elijah (1 Kings 19:21). Christ was called "'a minister of the sanctuary; that is, as our High Priest'" (Hebrews 8:2, Bible Dictionary 295). Jesus was minister of His Heavenly Father and it is in Him that we find a perfect model of a minister. And so it continues as "one generation shall command [His] works to another and declare [His] mighty acts" (Psalms 145:18).

The call to teach and have the words of God fully understood and heeded must remain in God's perspective.

The Lord's perspective is learned through the study of Scripture. "All Scripture is breathed out by God and profitable for teaching, for reproof, for correction, and for training in righteousness that the man of God may be competent, equipped for every good work" (1 Timothy 3:16). His words are the same yesterday, today and in the future (Heb. 13:8). Jesus adds in the book of Revelation, "I warn everyone who hears the words of the prophecy of this book. If anyone adds to them, God will add to him the plagues described in this book, and if anyone takes away for the words of the book of this prophecy, God will take away his share in the tree of life and in the holy city, which are described in this book" (22:18-19).

To that end, words and meanings are not to be altered. In Deuteronomy 8:3 the importance of words and their meanings are described as the following, "And he humbled you and let you hunger and fed you manna, which you did not know, nor did your fathers know, that he might make you know that man does not live by bread alone, but *man lives by every word that comes from the mouth of the*

Lord" (my emphasis). Later Jesus actualized the verses when He was tested by Satan after forty days of fasting and praying in the wilderness. Satan tried to tempt Jesus to prove that he is the Son of God by turning stones into loaves of bread. Jesus answered him, "It is written, 'Man shall not live by bread alone, but by every word that comes out from the mouth of God" (Matthew 4:4). Jesus was faithful to the words of His Father.

The term word is used multiple times in Scripture. The Greek counterpart is "logos" which is translated to mean word or reason. In the book of John, logos or word is used as a proper noun for Jesus and also another name for the gospel (Bible Dictionary and Concordance).

In the beginning was the Word, and the Word was with God, and the Word was God. He was in the beginning with God. All things were made through him, and without him was not anything made that was made. In him was life, and the life was the light of men. The light shines in the darkness, and the darkness has not overcome it. The true light, which enlightens everyone, was coming into the world. (John 1:1-5).

The Word that is Jesus Christ is the origin from whence being is sourced and Who came to live among man. The man - God brought a new beginning for humanity and a new perspective of reality. Where once man lived in darkness and death and unaware of truth, Jesus provided the path out of darkness into truth and light. The light illuminated man's consciousness whereby he viewed his world from a true foundation in his Creator. Thus, the language man spoke was rooted in the new consciousness.

Paul, the apostles and prophets were elected to spread the good news of salvation to all. Those who hear and believe could also partake in the wonderful illumination, life and truth through Jesus Christ. With humbleness in heart (possibly recalling his former self), Paul claims the office of minister as a "gift of God's grace" (Ephesians 3:7). Paul understood the meaning of the office of minister, he grasped the significance of the "plan of the mystery hidden for ages in God who created all things" (Ephesians 3:9).

To assist the minister of Christ, Jesus promised a Helper. "You will receive power when the Holy Spirit has come upon you, and you will be my witness in Jerusalem and in all Judea and Samaria, and to the ends of the earth" (Acts 1:8). Jesus is stating that although He is not here physically, the Holy Spirit will be in His stead. "These things I have spoken to you while I am still with you. But the Helper, the Holy Spirit whom the Father will send in my name, he will teach you all things and bring to your remembrance all that I have said"' (John. 14:25-26). The Holy Spirit will give to all who believe the words that need to be spoken.

In the letter to the church of Ephesus, Paul writes,

When you read this, you can perceive my insight into the *mystery* of Christ which was not made known to the sons of men in other generations as it is now been revealed to his fellow apostles and prophets by the Spirit. This mystery is that the

Gentiles are fellow heirs, members of the same body and partakers of the promises in Christ Jesus through the gospel. Of this gospel I was made minister according the gifts of God's grace, which was given to me by the working of his power. To me, though I am the very least of all saints, his grace was given to preach to the Gentiles the unsearchable riches of Christ, and to bring to light for everyone what is the plan of the *mystery* hidden for ages in God who created all things, so that through the church the manifold wisdom of God might now be made known to the rulers and authorities in the heavenly places. This is according to the eternal purpose that he realized in Christ Jesus our Lord, in whom we have boldness and access with confidence through faith (3:4-12, my emphasis).

The word mystery used in the New Testament means "a spiritual truth which cannot be discovered by mere reasons, but which is revealed, although its full comprehension is beyond our finite understanding" (Bible Dictionary, 303).

For the first time in human history, the mystery of Christ, the meaning of Jesus Christ is made known by the indwelling Holy Spirit. Through the Holy Spirit, the meaning of Jesus Christ is perpetuated from merely head knowledge to a transcendent and potentially actualized state of being. The mystery of the Gospel is the great plan of God for the salvation of the Jews and Gentiles alike. By comprehending all these things Paul was able to "bring to light for everyone the plan of the mystery" by careful articulation inspired by the Holy Spirit.

The careful choosing of words rooted in the being of Jesus Christ is important. The words grow the Church so that the church as a corporate body of believers manifest the wisdom of God. Words are the method to unite the church "to equip the saints for the work of ministry, for building up the Body of Christ, until we all attain to the unity of faith and of the knowledge of the Son of God, to mature manhood, to the measure of the fullness of Christ, so that we many no longer be children tossed to and fro by waves and carried about by every wind of doctrine by human cunning, by craftiness in deceitful schemes" (Ephesians 4:12-14). "This is according to the eternal purposes that he [God] realized in Christ Jesus our Lord" in order that we have assurance and courage through faith (Ephesians 3:11).

Paul warns us that "even Satan disguises himself as an angel of light. So it is no surprise if his servants [messengers/angels] also disguise themselves as servants [messengers/angels] of righteousness" (2 Corinthians 11:14). When God's plan was made known "to the sons of man in other generations" both the good angels and bad angels were informed as well as "rulers and authorities in the heavenly places" (Ephesians 3:5, 10). Paul states later in his letter to the Ephesians, "For we do not wrestle against flesh and blood, but against the rulers, against authorities, against the cosmic powers over this present darkness, against spiritual forces of evil in heavenly places" (3:10, 6:12).

The battle is on. No longer will the fight be a physical one as demonstrated in the Old Testament where a plethora of clashes are described. The dawning of the Gospel (the revealed mystery; the plan) changed the mechanics of war from the physical realm to the spiritual one. "But as it is, Christ attained a ministry that is much more excellent than the old as the covenant he mediates is better since it is enacted on better promises" (Hebrews 8:6).

As such, the stakes are higher. Better covenant, better promises. Satan's head must be exploding. Jesus describes Satan as "a murderer from the beginning, and has nothing to do with truth, because there is no truth in him. When he lies, he speaks out of his own character, for he is a liar, and the father of lies" (John 8:44).

In the parable of the sower, Jesus described the word as a seed. In Luke 8:11-12, He states, "Now the parable is this: The seed is the word of God. The ones along the path are those who have heard; then the devil comes and takes away the word from their hearts, so that they may not believe and be saved." Satan desperately tries to snatch the seed, that is, the word which was spoken to the listener. He understands that "if you confess with your mouth that Jesus is Lord and believe in your heart that God raised Him from the dead, you will be saved" (Romans 10:10). When one listens to a minister of the Lord and studies Scripture, faith grows (Romans 10:17).

Speaking and hearing are instrumental in God's plan for salvation. The word proclaimed "day to day pours out speech, and night to night reveals knowledge. There is no speech, nor are there words, whose voice is not heard. The voice goes out through all the earth, and their words to the ends of the world" (Psalms 19:2-4). To achieve this purpose, there must be comprehension by the hearer. If the hearer cannot understand the minister of the Lord who will speak to reveal the mystery of Christ, all is lost. Jesus says, "Behold, I stand at the door, and knock. If anyone hears my voice and opens, I will come in to him and eat with him and he with me". (Revelation 3:20).

Consider this. One can assume that the word of God has gone to ends of the earth as stated in Psalm 19. There is no excuse because of God's written word, the Bible. Through Scripture, one begins to form an understanding or conceive a model of Jesus exemplified through His actions and spoken words. There is confidence in these words and deeds because they never change (Hebrews 13:8). But today, most agree that society is defined by postmodernism that embraces change in every aspect and institution of society, including language. Therefore, if Jesus comes knocking on the door of the unsaved person's heart, the person may ask "Who is there?" Jesus will respond in His usual steadfast way. But will the person understand Him?

The answer is doubtful. Satan can certainly work on man by distorting the meaning, if not totally change the perspective of the word. Confusion is evidenced in the myriad of church denominations that exist today. Not only is there disagreement corporately but also individually. Can Christianity agree on "one God, one baptism, one faith" (Ephesians 4:5)? There are as many denominations in operation as there are interpretations of Scripture. Kinnaman asserts that presently we are "living in tension." He writes,

The digital revolution, endemic social change, and a shifting narrative of faith in our culture has deeply affected the cognitive and emotional process of 'encoding' faith. Because of *access, alienation,* and *authority,* the ability of one generation to convey the message and meaning of faith to the next generation-in thought forms, ideas, and practices they can readily understand and incorporate in their lives- has been disrupted (56).

True, the meaning of words change as years go by according to societal shifts. Today, the Good News (the Gospel) is hampered by preachers/ministers not revealing the whole truth, focusing on self and distrusting any authoritative figure or stance. The words, though, that are contained in Scripture do not change for they are timeless. Christians continue to use these words with their associated absolute meaning. But of late, words that Christians use to convey the life giving message are not received by the hearers. Going back four generations in American culture, the following example illustrates the change.

Elders used words like these: World War II and the Depression; 'smarter,' 'honest,' 'work ethic,' and 'values and morals'…Boomers describe their generation with terms like 'work ethic,' respectful,' values and morals, and 'smarter.' Busters use these terms with 'technology use,' 'work ethic,' 'conservative/tradition,' 'smarter' and 'respectful'…The Millennials use these five phrases to describe their generation: 'technology use,' music and pop culture,' 'liberal/tolerant,' smarter' and 'clothes.' Where has the respectful gone? Where is *work ethic*? To me [Kinnaman], this shows that the next generation is not just sort of different; they are discontinuously different (Kinnaman 37-38).

There is a powerful realization that in a matter of a century, priorities have shuffled, if not dropped and as I hope to demonstrate, meanings to words have been shifted also. Meanings of words, void of the God given one, takes on the spirit of the world. In doing so, the person who hears words empty of its God given meaning, allows entry for the secular meaning. If the secular meaning is received by the person, that person will not "understand the things freely given to us by God" (1 Corinthians 2:12). Instead of imparting the wisdom as taught by the Holy Spirit, humanist wisdom is passed on. Thus man is kept in a natural/physical state and opposed to a spiritual state enlightened by the Holy Spirit. "For those who live according to the flesh [natural] set their minds on the things of the flesh [natural], but those who live according to the Spirit set their minds on the Spirit... For the mind set on the flesh [natural] is hostile to God" (Romans 8:5, 7). "The natural person does not accept the things of the Spirit of God, for they are folly to him and he is not able to understand them because they are spiritually discerned"

(1 Corinthians. 2:14). If the Spirit of God is not present in man, he cannot spiritually distinguish what is of God and what is not because he relies on his abilities. His abilities are finite and flawed. They are no match against the schemes of the devil (Ephesians 6:11). Therefore, mankind

is indeed doomed unless Christians understand the dire state of affairs for mankind.

If this pivotal strategy of the evil one is carried out, that is, changing the meanings of words thereby the societal perspective, a domino effect will ensue, most dangerously in the churches. Starting with the Gospel, if the meanings are changed, the truth will be hidden. If the truth is hidden, the mystery of God's plan is not known which means no salvation for humanity. Church history attests to the resultant myriad of church denominations present today evidenced by the fracturing of the faith because of numerous interpretations of Scripture (Osso *Synthesis*). Since the turn of the 20th century, the source of the message taught in churches does not find its bearing in Scripture but in culture.

An example of this phenomenon is with Darwin's theory of evolution. Suddenly a discussion about the origin of man and all living creatures is raised, doubting God's word on creation. The trajectory of man's source of being, knowledge and understanding drastically shifted from a vertical one with God as the source to a horizontal one where cultural sentiments prevail. Words which are commonly used in conveying the Gospel have their meanings now dictated by culture. Eventually a false gospel is communicated. Is this not what the Bible warns us about? Jude writes in his letter to the faithful, "But you must remember, beloved, the predictions of the apostles of our Lord Jesus Christ. They said to you, 'In the last time there will be scoffers, following their own ungodly passions.' It is these who cause divisions, worldly people, devoid of the Spirit" (17-18). "As [Jesus] sat on the Mount of Olives, the disciples came to Him privately, saying, 'Tell us, when will these things be, and what will be the sign of your coming and the close of the age?' And Jesus answered them,' See that no one leads you astray. For many will come in my name, saying 'I am the Christ and they will lead many astray'" (Matthew 24:1-5).

The unwavering thesis is that Jesus is the same yesterday, today and forever yet man is increasingly taken into sensuality (the antithesis). For example, turn on the television and 99% of the content contains some form of carnality; their core gospel being to follow the heart. "The heart [though] is deceitful above all things and desperately sick, who can understand it?" (Jeremiah 17.9) Nevertheless, through God's grace and mercy, He promises to write His word on our hearts (Romans 5:5; 6:17, Hebrews 10:22; 1 John 3:21). The meaning of a word is like the spirit of the word, its essence, the substance or being of the word. When a word is spoken, the hearer discerns its meaning, its spirit. If the meaning of the word is changed, then the spirit of the word is changed also. The hearer has the option to accept or reject the word based on its meaning and spirit. The simple truth is that words void of God (which would inherently possess a good spirit) will take on a secular meaning (a spirit not linked with God but with the other). A case in point is the word sin. Sin is defined as breaking God's law; rebellion against His law.

First John 3:4 describes sin as lawlessness. Today sin no longer represents lawlessness. "The reason, of course, is that we have lost the moral world in which sin is alone understood. The religious authorities who once gave us rules for life and who gave us the metaphysical world in which those rules found their grounding have all faded in our moral imaginations. Today, we are more alone in this world than any previous generation" (Wells 37).

Through the tenet of pluralism and relativism which have become strongholds in today's society the word sin no longer has the meaning and spirit as in the previous generations. How is raw American individualism and the heresy of Pelagianism, which asserts that people are born innocent of sin, that sin is a set of bad practices that is caught later on in life rather like a disease? Believers stand alone because the absolute truths taught to us, the unchanging word of God, have been compromised by the transformation of meaning and spirit to a secular one.

The consequence is that we have come to believe that the self retains its access to the sacred, an access not ruptured by sin. In 2002, a national survey by Barna turned up the astonishing discovery that despite all the difficulties that modernized life has created, despite its rapaciousness, greed and violence, 74% of those surveyed rejected the idea of original sin and 52% of evangelicals concurred. These were the percentages of respondents who agreed with the statement that 'when people are born they are neither good nor evil-they make a choice between the two as they mature (Wells 37).

Indeed, people continue to pick and choose at will. What happens then, when what is supposed to be good is really bad and what is meant for bad is really good? (Wells 37). Man has allowed Satan to hijack the basic doctrine of sin which sets in motion the process towards salvation when convicted! Sin is no longer a form of rebellion and lawlessness but now considered a disease. Try explaining sin as defined in Scripture to an unbeliever and he/she might respond with something like, "Take two aspirins and you will be cured."

Language in Theology

Jonah 1:1 states, "Now the word of the Lord came to Jonah the son of Amittai, saying, 'Arise, go to Nineveh, that great city, and call out against it, for their evil has come up before Me. '"God commanded Jonah to speak to the people of Nineveh and convict them of their evil ways. Jonah could only do this through language, choosing the words that succinctly communicated the message of God. He would have had, as a prerequisite to follow God's command, a mastery of the Ninevite language and the Assyrian culture. Jonah may have wondered how he was to communicate to a pagan society with its warring factions. Considering the options, he chose to run the other way, away from Nineveh negating God's mandate (1:3). Nevertheless, God showed compassion by forgiving Jonah for fleeing. "Then the Lord came to Jonah the second time, 'Arise, go to Nineveh, that great city, and call out against it the message I tell you.' Jonah obeyed and when word reached the King of Nineveh that God spoke, he proclaimed, 'Let everyone turn from his evil ways and from violence that is in his hands'" (3:6,8). The words of the Lord are powerful and no one should doubt its life changing effect.

In the New Testament, Jesus is chronicled as having actualized what Jonah should have done. Jesus came into this world, participating fully in the culture, using their language in order to fulfill the will of His Father. Human language as a construct of society, although imperfect, is a way God uses for His purposes.

God uses words in the service of his intention to rescue men and women, drawing them into fellowship with Him and preparing a new creation as an appropriate venue for the enjoyment of that fellowship. In other words, the knowledge of God that is the goal of God's speaking ought never to be separated from the centerpiece of Christian theology; namely, the salvation of sinners (Thompson in Keller 110).

Being an integral part in the ministry of the Kingdom of God, language is therefore, used for,

1. Judgment – the words that come out of each individual will be adjudicated accordingly.

    "I tell you, on the day of judgment people will give account for every careless word they speak, for by your words you will be condemned" (Matthew 12:36-37).

2. Spreading the Gospel – the good news is revealed to others through language inspired by the Holy Spirit.

    "For I am not ashamed of the gospel, for it is the power of God for salvation to everyone who believes, to the Jew first and also to the Greek. For in it the righteousness of God is revealed from faith for faith, as it is written, 'The righteous shall live by faith" *(Romans 1:16-17).*

3. Power – there is authority in the words of the Lord and to those who use it according to His will.

    Then he said to me, 'Prophesy over these bones, and say to them, O dry bones, hear the word of the Lord.'

Thus says the Lord God to these bones: 'Behold, I will cause breath to enter you, and you shall live. And I will lay sinews upon you, and will cause flesh to come to you, and cover you with skin, and put breath in you, and you shall live, and you shall know that I am Lord.' So I prophesied as I was commanded. And as I prophesied, there was a sound, and behold, a rattling, and the bones came together, bone to its bone. And I looked, and behold, there were sinews on them, and flesh had come upon them, and skin had covered them. But there was no breath. Then he said to me, 'Prophesy to the breath; prophesy, son of man, and say to the breath, Thus says the Lord God: Come from the four winds, O breath, and breathe on these slain, that they may live.' So I prophesied as he commanded me, and the breath came into them, and they lived and stood on their feet, and exceedingly great army (Ezekiel 37:4-10).

"*He said to them, 'Because of your little faith. For truly I say to you, if you have faith, like a grain of* mustard seed, you will say to this mountain, 'Move from here to there,' and it will move, and nothing will be impossible for you" (Matthew 17:20).

4. Asserting absolute truth that is rooted in Jesus Christ.

    "Sanctify them in truth; my word is truth. As you sent me into the world, so I have sent them into the world. And for their sake I consecrate myself, that they also may be sanctified in truth" (John 17:17-19).

5. Edification of conduct – The book of Proverbs contains eleven passages that address the spoken word and listening.

    "The lips of the righteous know what is acceptable, but the mouth of the wicked, what is perverse" (10:32).

    "There is one whose rash words are like sword thrust, but the tongue of the wise is healing" (12:18).

    "A wise son hears his father's instruction, but a scoffer does not listen to rebuke" (13:1).

"Whoever guards his mouth preserves his life; he who opens wide his lips comes to ruin" (13:3).

"By insolence comes nothing but strife, but with those who take advice is wisdom" (13:10).

"Poverty and grace come to him who ignores instruction, but whoever heeds reproof is honored" (13:18).

"By the mouth of the fool comes a rod for his back, but the lips of the wise will preserve them" (14:3).

"Leave the presence of a fool, for there you do not meet words of knowledge" (14:7).

"In all the toil there is profit, but mere talk tends only to poverty" (14:23).

"A truthful witness saves lives, but one who breathes out lies is deceitful" (14:25).

"A soft answer turns away wrath, but a harsh word stirs up anger" (15:1).

(Poythress).

Just as language is important in the ministry of God, it is primary in the work of Satan. To comprehend the extent language can be used to advance the role of Satan in the life of humanity, one only has to review the happenings during World War II (1939-1945). Noted in the book of Genesis, language as a construct of society, is a gift of God. Also recorded throughout Scripture is the fallen state of man and his proneness to sin. World War II exemplifies the depth of man's depraved nature with Adolf Hitler, dictator of Germany during this period, taking first prize. In Hitler's warped mind to establish himself as ruler of the world, his plan was to reorganize society through propaganda, intimidation and bloodshed (Osso *Superficial Society*). His deceitful plan started first with his fellow Germans.

The German Christians' Conference was a disturbing spectacle for anyone wary of Hitler's zeal to reorder German society. The lines between church and state were being blurred aggressively. It was one thing where the state was led by the Christian Kaiser, but another when it was led by the anti-Christian Fuhrer. Most Germans believed

Hitler was basically 'one of them' however, and they welcomed the Nazi's plans to reorder society, including the church. Herman Goring gave a speech to great acclaim, casting the reordering of society as mainly an 'administrative' change'....The German Christians wanted a unified German church in accord with Nazi principles, and they fought toward that end. If England could have a Church of England, why shouldn't Germany have its own church, too – and on firmly 'German' foundation? (Metaxas 157).

The consequences of reordering society was felt by many German Christians. In the reorganization, language was also altered.

German Christians spoke of baptism as a baptism not into the body of Christ but into the 'community of the *Volk* and into the *Weltanschauug* of the Fuhrer. Communion presented other difficulties. One pastor spoke of the bread symbolizing 'the body of the earth that, firm and strong, remains true to the German soil,' and the wine was the 'blood of the earth.' The paganism of it all escaped them (Metaxas 173).

Indeed, paganism escaped the German people because meanings had been changed.

Today, speech is determined by employing Hegelian dialect which basically is an aberrant logic that is counter to anything of God. According to this logic, the tension between being and non-being creates a synthesis of both. The tenets of the logic undermine absolution, exclusiveness and authority. The logic continues with the newly created synthesis, looking to its opposite for progression in being. The logic dictates that for anything to have being, it must look to its opposite. The process repeats itself over and over till what is believed, perfection occurs.

Such reasoning is used in all aspects of life including human history (Osso Synthesis). An example excerpted from the book, *The Monstrosity of Christ. Paradox or Dialectic?* by Slavoz Zizek and John Milbank and edited by Creston Davis, demonstrates its application to Christian theology. (Please note that Zizek is an atheist, Marxist philosopher and psychoanalyst. Milbank is a contemporary Christian theologian. I find it offensive that an atheist has the audacity to preach to Christians what Christianity should be and furthermore that Christian theologians would even consider what they have to say in regards to the faith!) In the chapter entitled, "The Fear of Four Words: A Modest Pleas For the Hegelian Reading of Christianity," Zizek writes,

> What he [C. K. Chesterton] doesn't get is that *universal(ized)* is no longer a crime – it sublates *(negates/overcomes) itself as crime and turns from transgression into a new order.* He is right to claim that, compared to the 'entirely lawless' philosopher, burglars, bigamists, murderers even, are essentially moral: thief is a 'conditionally good man,' he doesn't deny property as such, he just wants more of it for himself, and is quite ready to respect it. The conclusion to be drawn from this, however, is that crime is 'essentially moral' that it simply wants a

particular illegal reordering of a global moral order which should remain. And, in a truly Hegelian spirit, we should bring this proposition (of the 'essential morality' of the crime) to its immanent reversal: not only is crime 'essentially moral' (in Hegelese: an inherent moment of deployment of the inner antagonisms and 'contradictions' of the very notion of moral order, not something that disturbs moral order, not something that disturbs moral order from outside, as an accidental intrusion) but *morality itself is essentially criminal* – again, not only in the sense that the more radically moral order necessarily 'negates itself' in particular crimes, but, more radically, in the sense that *the way morality (in the case theft, property) asserts itself is already a crime)* – 'property is theft' as they used to say in the nineteenth century. That is to say, one should pass from theft as a particular crime to a violation of the universal form of property to this form itself as a criminal violation (44-45).

The aforementioned excerpt is an example of language and meaning that is not grounded in Scripture but in a certain philosopher by the name of Georg Wilhelm Friedrich Hegel (1770-1831, the Romantic Period of philosophy). This type of Hegelian logic or dialect is increasing in popularity particularly in Christian circles whose sentiments lie in Radical Orthodoxy. (To me, it is a mind boggling reversal of western logic that has its bearings in Christian metaphysical philosophy. The whole of which, Satan who cannot devise anything original except for lies, takes logic as is commonly known and reverses it. What is good is now considered bad, and what is bad is now deemed good).

Beginning in the early 1990's in the halls of Cambridge University, Great Britain, Radical Orthodoxy is finding its way across the Atlantic Ocean as a theological movement particularly in the ecumenical realm. The theological movement is based on the tension between postmodernism and the writings of Catholic Church fathers from the medieval era of church history. "The core belief of Radical Orthodoxy is that there is no 'autonomous reality.' Namely, there is no such entity as a self-directing, 'in-itself existence.' Rather, every aspect of created reality is only insofar as it participates in the Creator" (Smith, 16). Radical Orthodoxy's stance endeavors to dissect,

> All reality [to] participate[s] in the transcendent. Radical Orthodoxy also affirms every realm of human vocation as a site for the mediation of such transcendence. Hence, the studies in *Radical Orthodoxy: A New Theology* grapple with core aspects of human-in-the-world: language, friendship, sex, embodiment, politics, and communal life, art and music. The goal of the project is 'to re-envisage particular cultural spheres from a theological perspective which they all regard as the only non-nihilistic perspective, and only the perspective able to uphold even finite reality (Smith 17-18).

Radical Orthodoxy's (RO) stance sounds reasonable but at its heart, it seeks to reconcile the world through an association of common core ideals and disputes among

Reformed theology. The way to achieve that end is to go back to church tradition. The claim made is to study what the Holy Spirit revealed to the church patria (Smith). Really? Are there more works other than the Holy Bible that were undoubtedly inspired by the Holy Spirit? RO pretends to eschew all that postmodernism has to offer yet embraces social theories set forth by such atheist social scientists as Herbert Marcuse, Walter Benjamin, Walter Habermas, all critical theorists as well. (Osso, *Superficial Society*). RO can serve one purpose and that is to demonstrate how men and women gifted with intellect to serve the Lord swerve off course. Instead of discerning current events through a Christological perspective, ecclesiological traditions are used as a measure.

Didn't Jesus say in the book of Revelation, "I warn everyone who hears the words of the prophesy of this book: if anyone adds to them, God will add to him the plagues described in this book, and if anyone takes away from the words of the book of this prophecy, God will take away his share in the tree of life and in the holy city, which are described in this book" (22:18)?

Summary

Recent research has determined that the current generation is "discontinuously different" than previous generations. Rapid cultural shifts today have caused an intergenerational disconnect. Variables in cultural shifts have been identified through a recent Barna Research by David Kinnaman. They are the digitalization of society, endemic social change, and the corresponding shift of beliefs within the Christian faith. The effects of which make it difficult for the transfer of faith from one generation to another. The response to Christianity as it is presented today is met with confusion and a lack of understanding. The general reply of the present generation upon hearing the Good News is, "Wait, I don't understand. You lost me."

The contention proposed is that the language that is used to bring the message of the Good News to the new generation is no longer understood. Although words that are spoken have not changed, the meaning has, and to one that is not rooted in God. There exists a language within language. Meanings of words can also be expressed as the spirit of the word. If the meaning or spirit of the word is empty of God then secular meaning and spirit fill its void. This process is identified as a strategy of Satan to keep mankind in darkness with its goal to lead man to its demise.

Language has been demonstrated through Scripture as essential for the ministry of God's word. Five uses for language were identified. The uses are for judgment (Matthew 12:36-37), spreading the Gospel (Romans 1:16-17), power (Ezekiel 37:4-10, Matthew 17:20), assertion of absolute truth rooted in Jesus Christ (John 17:17-19) and edification of conduct (Proverbs 10:32, 12:18, 13:3,10,18,14:3, 7,23,25, 15:1). If the spoken word of ministers, inspired by the Holy Spirit is not understood, the mystery of Christ as partakers of the promises of the Lord will seem folly to the hearers. Salvation is blocked and mankind is headed towards destruction. Hegelian dialect has been identified as the logic behind the spoken language.

Radical Orthodoxy is cited as an example of its use in Christian theology. The spread of Hegelian logic is widespread and may account for the disparity between the present and former generations. To that end, one needs to ask, "When Jesus comes knocking on the door of someone's heart, will the person understand Him when He calls out to him/her?"

I.   GOD AS THE AUTHOR OF LANGUAGE

In the beginning man was linked with one language. This is documented in Genesis 11:1 which states, "Now the whole earth had one language and the same words." In the book of Exodus, Moses questioned his ability to address Pharaoh and petition him to free the nation of Israel. God responded with the following, "Who has made man's mouth? Who made him mute, or deaf, or seeing or blind? Is it not I, the Lord?" (Exodus 4:11). The Lord asserts Himself as the author of language.

The earliest passages of Scripture state, "And God *said,* 'Let there be light and there was light'... And God *said,* 'Let there be an expanse in the midst of the waters, and let it separate the waters from the waters'.... And God *called* the expanse Heaven. And there was evening and there was morning" (Genesis 1:3, 7, 8, my emphasis). As God spoke, His words went forth and the world came into being. What power and majesty is generated by the speech of God! The world was literally formed by God's words. Through His words, creation received life and being (meaning). "Worthy are you, our Lord and God, to receive glory and honor and power, for you created all things, and by your will they existed and were created" (Revelation 4:11). Therefore, the whole of creation is linked to the meaning of God's spoken word which gives it life.

In the New Testament, life existed in the words spoken by Jesus. Simon Peter questioned Him asking "Lord, to whom shall we go? You have the words of *eternal life*" (John 6:68, my emphasis). It wasn't till the Savior gave up His life to pay the penalty for man's sin and resurrection that His disciples and eventually others began to understand. With the Helper, the Holy Spirit, the world made sense. Today His disciples are compelled to, "Go and stand in the temple and speak to the people all the words of this *life*" (Acts 5:20, my emphasis). Throughout the history of mankind, man's search for meaning holds the key to understanding history and emerging events (Poythress).

The Purpose of Language

In Genesis 1:28, God says to Adam and Eve, "Be fruitful and multiply and fill the earth and subdue it and have dominion over the fish and every living thing that moves on the earth." The manner in which God spoke to the original humans implies the pair already understood God's language. It appears that God had already "programmed" them or set in their genetic makeup, the ability to understand God's speech when He spoke. It could simply be that God created man in His own image, therefore instinctly understood God.

Continuing in Genesis 2:19-20, Adam is called upon to use his gift of language.

> Now out of the ground the Lord God had formed every beast of the field and every bird of the heavens and brought them to the man to see what he would call them. And whatever the man called

every living creature, that was its name. The man gave names to all livestock and to the birds of the heavens and to every beast of the field.

Genesis 2:23 provides the first written record of Adam's words uttered, "'This at last is bone of my bones and flesh of my flesh; she shall be called Woman, because she was taken out of Man.'" Assumption can be made that Adam was speaking to God and not to Eve. In the perfect paradise of the Garden of Eden, all of man's words and deeds were done to glorify God. Because God is the Creator of all things, the purpose of language, is to glorify Him (Grudem). Isaiah 43:7 confirms that language is to praise Him by stating, "Everyone who is called by my name, whom I created for my glory, whom I formed and made." In chapter three of Genesis, an interaction between Adam, Eve and God is recorded. At this point, logic and human thought are introduced with the use of language. "The man said, 'The woman whom you gave to be with me, she gave me fruit of the tree, and I ate.' Then the Lord God said to the woman, 'What is this that you have done?' The woman said, 'The serpent deceived me, and I ate'" (12-13).

Dr. Vern Poythress, professor of New Testament interpretation at Westminster Theological Seminary in Philadelphia, Pa. maintains that language is manifested through the triune God. Taking the three attributes of God which are omniscience, omnipotence and omnipresence, Poythress parcels them out to the three Persons of God. God the Father is reflected in omniscience as the One who illuminates or gives meaning. He is, therefore, the source of meaning as the Divine Creator.

God the Son is revealed in omnipotence as the Son who responds to God's command for the light to exist. God becomes man through Jesus and through Him, God's actualizes His plan for man's redemption. The third person of God is the Spirit and is mirrored in the omnipresence of God. Through the Spirit, God reveals Himself in His integrity, strength, and purity of light (*In The Beginning Was the Word* 27). He is with us.

I wholeheartedly agree in the three attributes of the Lord as omniscience, omnipotent and omnipresent. But I humbly disagree in some areas how these attributes disclose themselves through language to mankind. Since language's intent is to glorify God, there has to be a symbiotic process between God and man. God speaks to man and man responds to God and vice versa. The following is a proposal of this glorious process that takes place by faith in Jesus. Jesus in one's life is imperative for this process to take place since He is the One who opens the door to God that was once shut by sin.

God the Father as the Source of Meaning

God as all– knowing (omniscience) gives us knowledge and meaning as He clarifies our call from Him to us. "Your word is a lamp to my feet and a light to my path" (Psalm 119:105). His words illuminate by shedding light on the world in order to provide knowledge and wisdom. In respect to meaning, a deeper understanding is needed. The Lord is always looking "down from heaven on the children of man, to see if there are any who understand, who seek after God" (Psalm 14:2). From an existential perspective, meaning takes on the fullness of God's language and transcends it through time and space. In the previous chapter, the meaning of words was discussed as having a spirit which permeates each word. The contention continues to be assumed in this chapter as well. Thus, when meaning is mentioned, the spirit of the word is also surmised. The placement of meaning in the spiritual allows it to bypass the interference of generational and/or sociological variances and time.

In other words, meaning that emanates from God and viewed on a transcendental plane is not yoked with humanistic interpretations. From the beginning of time when God spoke, the earth and all of creation were formed as well as their purpose. Therefore, their meaning is forever bound to their Creator. Nothing has changed since the birth of things. God exists and He continues to call in the same language He used to create the foundations of the earth. Hence, humanity finds its being, worth and purpose in God. God's language provides definition in the following way.

1. He made man in His image.

   Then God said, 'Let *us* make man in *our* image, after *our* likeness. And let them have dominion over the fish of the sea and over the birds of the heavens and over the livestock and over all the earth and over every creeping thing that creeps on the earth.' So God created man in his own image, in the image of God he created him; male and female he created them. Then the Lord God formed the man of dust from the ground and breathed into his nostrils the breath of life, and the man became a living creature (Genesis 1:26-27, 2:7, my emphasis).

(Note that God's statement of "us" and "our" signifies the inclusion of God the Son and God the Holy Spirit. The triune God participates in creation). The creation of man in God's image sets man apart from His other creations. He exalts man above all by bestowing him with dominion over all other creation. God places in man some characteristics of Himself namely logic, language, morality, love, responsibility and creativity (ESV Study Bible).

2. Human existence rests on the fact that man is meaningful to Him. Therefore, man derives worth and meaning from God (Grudem). Jesus stated in His high priestly prayer, "They [mankind] may all be one, just as you Father are in me, and I in you, that they [mankind] also may be in us" (John 17:21). "And I will be a father to you, and you will be sons and daughters to me, says the Lord Almighty" (2 Corinthians 6:18).

Humanity is not only defined but related to God as sons and daughters who as children, should look to Him for guidance, knowledge, comfort, wisdom, security and protection. The interaction between the children and Father is facilitated through communication by way of His language. (Take care at this point not to interpret this as God being an overbearing God). God's original intent for creation was to bring Him joy, delight and honor. Then man disobeyed condemning all creation into the bondage of darkness. Needless to say, God's love for man has not diminished and through Isaiah, God tells us His will for the restoration of His people. "You shall be a crown of beauty in the hand of the Lord, and a royal diadem in the hand of your God. You shall no more be termed, Forsaken, and your land shall no more be termed Desolate, but you shall be called My Delight is in Her, and your land Married; for the Lord delights in you, and your land shall be married" (62: 3-5).

As sons and daughters of God the Father, our language then, should reflect that relationship. "Let the words of my mouth and the mediation of my heart be acceptable in your sight, O Lord, my rock and my redeemer" (Isaiah 19:14). God's response, "Heaven and earth will pass away, but my words will not pass" (Matthew 24:35).

God the Son as Unity

As previously stated, in the beginning there was only one language given to man as a gift from God. Language serves to unite man with God as well as to glorify

Him. "God himself is a *unity*. A unified and completely integrated whole person who is infinitely perfect" (Grudem 180). Man was supposed to live in the Garden of Eden in blissful union with God. But in Genesis 11:1-9 man's plot to join together against God and prove that man did not need Him is recorded as well as the consequences.

> Now the whole earth had one language and the same words. And as people migrated from the east, they found a plain in the land of Shinar and settled there. And they said to one another, 'Come, let us make bricks, and burn them thoroughly.' And they had brick for stone, and bitumen for mortar. Then they said, 'Come, let us build ourselves a city and a tower with its tip in the heavens, and let us make a name for ourselves, lest we be dispersed over the face of the whole earth. And the Lord came down to see the city and the tower, which the children of man built. And the Lord said, 'Behold, they are one people, and they have all one language, and this is only the beginning for them. Come, let *us* go down and there confuse their language, so that they may

not understand one another's speech. So the Lord dispersed them from there over the face of the earth, and they left off building the city. There its name was called Babel, because there the Lord confused the language of the earth. And from there the Lord dispersed them over the face of the earth (my emphasis).

The depicted situation demonstrates an attempt of humanity to be independent of God, proving that they are indeed self- sufficient. They knew they were disobeying God. They tried to outsmart God by first, "let us make a name for ourselves" (4). Why? "Lest we be dispersed over the face of the whole earth" (4). The people conspired to be known by a word or words that would be recognizable by them in case they had to disband or separate. God was not hoodwinked for He is perfect.

The people even deluded themselves to think that they could even be like God. Consequently, God (note "us", as in the Father, Son and Spirit) scattered them by changing the meaning of the one language that unified them, shattering their plot. They no longer could understand each other. Since they could not work together as one cohesive community, they left each other going in different directions. Hence the myriad of languages and dialects across the globe.

In the New Testament, God reveals His better covenant with man through His Son. Jesus is the means to unite mankind once again with God the Father. The letter to the church at Ephesus by Paul exemplifies Jesus as the Great Uniter. The letter "articulates general instructions in the truths of the cosmic redemptive work of God in Christ; *the unity of the church among diverse people;* and proper conduct in the church, the home, and the world. Unity and love in the bond of peace mark the work of the Savior as well as Christians' grateful response to free grace in their lives" (ESV Bible 2258, my emphasis).

Paul writes, "In him, we have redemption through his blood, the forgiveness of our trespasses, according to the riches of his grace, which he lavished upon us, in all wisdom and insight *making known* to us the mystery of his will, according to his purposes, which he set forth in Christ as *a plan for the fullness of time, to unite all things in Him,*

things in heaven and things on earth (1:7-10, my emphasis).
Paul is essentially saying that God's foremost strategy is to
restore all on earth and in heaven, uniting them via Jesus,
culminating at His second coming. Jesus broke the back of
sin that kept man and God apart when He came in the form
of man allowing for communication between God and man
as it was originally intended.

Man can once again pray, give thanksgiving and
praise to the Lord, worship, petition or simply talk to Him.
The Lord promises to listen. "If we know that He hears us
in whatever we ask, we know that we have the requests that
we have asked of Him" (1 John 5:15). "Therefore, I tell you,
whatever you ask in prayer, believe that you have received
it, and it will be yours" (Mark 11:24). As born again saints
unto God, listen out for God and understand His language
when He speaks. Comprehend Him when He "lavish [es]
upon us, in all wisdom and insight making known to us, the
mystery of his will" (Ephesians 1:8).

God calls upon each one of his people for a special
purpose. "His divine power has granted to all that pertain
to life and godliness, through the knowledge of him who

called us to his own glory and excellence, by which he has granted to us his precious and very great promises, so that through them you may become partakers of his nature" (1 Peter 1:3-4). In order to "become partakers of the divine nature," knowledge of the Almighty is foremost. The knowledge leads to understanding through the spoken Word. "There is no speech, nor are there words whose voice is not heard" (Psalm 19:3). But not all will understand. "For many are called, but few are chosen" (Matthew 22:14). Paul addresses the call of God by stating in the letter to the Ephesians the following:

> [I] urge you to walk in a manner worthy of the calling in which you have been called, with all humility and gentleness, with patience, bearing each with one another in love, eager to maintain the unity of the Spirit in the bond of peace. There is one body and one Spirit – just as you were called to the one hope that belongs to your call – one Lord, one faith, one baptism. One God and Father of all, who is over all and through all and in all (4:1-6).

The passage may describe the community/society in the Garden of Eden had not Adam and Eve not disobeyed the Lord. Indeed, the entire book of Ephesians is subdivided in sections that could provide a structure for a society according to the Lord's perspective. (How ironic. The answer to establish a true utopian society, studied by philosophers ad finitum, has been under their nose all the time if they only looked to God and opened a Bible). Beginning in chapter one, the topics are entitled "Spiritual Blessings in Christ, "Thanksgiving and Prayer." Chapter two is divided into "By Grace through Faith" and "One in Christ." Chapter three is composed of "The Mystery of the Gospel Revealed" and "Prayer for Spiritual Strength." Two parts comprise chapter four entitled "Unity in the Body of Christ" and "The New Life."

While chapter five is divided into "Walk in Love" and "Wives and Husbands," chapter six continues with "Children and Parents" and "The Whole Armor of God." The topics can be applied to form a framework for a godly society with all its constructs including language.

Following the prescription for a godly society, the rewards of such a society are great. They are:

1. Spiritual blessings in Christ. As adopted children of God established through Jesus Christ in God's redemptive plan, they inherit blessings, all to the praise of His glory.

2. Wisdom and knowledge. As a result of spiritual blessings, prayer and thanksgiving are to be continuously given unto God. Together as a body, a church praying as one with Jesus Christ as its head receives "wisdom and revelation in the knowledge of him" (Ephesians 1:17).

3. Grace through faith. By grace, man has been transformed from dead in sin to eternal life in Jesus Christ. Not by works but through faith, a gift of God, that is used to glorify Him.

4. The mystery of God revealed. In the passages of Ephesians Paul explains how he was sent by God to make known the Gospel to the Gentiles. Likewise, the Christian community is to do the same with

unbelievers. Believers possess the mystery of God in their hearts and must share it.

5. Spiritual strength. With Paul's prayer as a model, the Christian community prays for strength "with power through his Spirit in [everyone's] inner being" for an understanding of His will (3:16).

6. Unity in the body of Christ. The unity that binds all believers is "one Lord, one faith, one baptism" (Ephesians 4:5). The manner of which is displayed in humbleness, "gentleness with patience, bearing one another in love, eager to maintain the unity of the Spirit in the bond of peace" (Ephesians 4:2).

7. The new life. As followers of Christ, life is changed where minds are transformed and molded according to what was originally intended in the image of God.

8. Walk in love. As children of God, living is determined by the love we have for God and the desire to do His will. For the will of the Lord to be understood, the Holy Spirit is present. He prompts those who walk the path of love, humbleness

towards one another and thanksgiving to God in the name of Jesus Christ.

9. Husbands, wives and children. The ideal family unit as described in the letter to the Ephesians.

10. The whole armor of God. God provides all that is needed to stand firm against evilness.

The final topic in the book of Ephesians is "The Whole Armor of God." How superb is the role of the Almighty Father–God to end this book with a means to defend oneself against the enemy. Through Paul, God exhorts us to be "strong in the Lord and in the strength of his might. Put on the whole armor of God, that you may be able to stand against the schemes of the devil" (6:10).

In Paul's first letter to the Corinthians, he writes, "I appeal to you, brothers, by the name of our Lord Jesus Christ, that all of you agree, and that there be no divisions among you, but that you be united in the same mind and the same judgment" (1:10). How wonderful it is to live together in harmony sharing the common bond as children of God. Psalm 133 celebrates the beauty of a true Christian community.

Behold, how good and pleasant it is

when brothers dwell in unity!

It is like the precious oil on the head,

running down on the beard,

on the beard of Aaron,

running down on the collar of his robes!

It is like the dew of Hermon,

which falls on the mountains of Zion!

For there the Lord commanded the blessings,

Life forever.

In the psalm, happiness is first seen in Aaron who represents the priesthood. In the New Testament and today, the High Priest is Jesus Christ. Picture Jesus then, with oil (used on exclusive occasions and which symbolizes delight and pleasure) being anointed for the special occasion of being united into one body, His church. (Bible Dictionary).

Next a description of a physical place is given. The verse notes Mount Hermon, known for its dew and is located in the northern region of Israel. The mountains of Zion is a southwestern hill and is sometimes used to refer to Jerusalem (Bible Dictionary). In this particular place, God blesses it with eternal life. Envision this as the Christian community as well as God the Son and High Priest, rejoicing with each person who is saved. "The Lord your God is in your midst, a mighty one who will save; he will rejoice over you with gladness; he will quiet you by his love; he will exult over you with loud singing" (Zephaniah 3:17). "For the Lord takes pleasure in his people; he adorns the humble with salvation. Let the godly exult in glory; let them sing for joy on their beds" (Psalm 149:4-5).

God the Spirit as the Speaker

Romans 8:8-11 sets the foundation how God the Spirit and as the Speaker works in one's life. It states,

> Those who are in the flesh cannot please God. You, however, are not of the flesh but in the Spirit, if in fact the Spirit of God dwells in you. Anyone who does not have the Spirit of Christ does not belong to him. But if Christ is in you, although the body is dead because of sin, the Spirit is life because of righteousness. If the Spirit of him who raised Jesus

from the dead dwells in you, he who raised Christ

Jesus from the dead will also give life to your mortal

bodies through his Spirit who dwells in you.

The passage emphasizes that the state of one's relationship with the Lord is literally a matter of life or death. The mind that is in line with God will have eternal life. If not, the evil one will step in to wreak havoc and death. Herein lies the urgency of learning the vernacular language, the language within language of present society. If the current generation does not fathom the Good News, a whole generation of humanity is condemned to death. "For the word of the cross is folly to those who are perishing, but to us who are being saved it is the power of God" (1 Corinthians 1:18).

Pastor Dave Roberson hits the nail on its head when he defines the Holy Spirit in the context of language. In his book, entitled *The Walk of the Spirit. The Walk of Power,* Roberson writes,

Why did God send the Holy Spirit to live inside of

you? So He could change you into the image of His

Son. And in order to accomplish that goal, the Holy

Spirit brought His own prayer language with Him so He could pray for all that concerns you. With that prayer language, He gets involved directly with you in a one-on-one relationship that is independent of anyone else, even of your mind… Every time you give the Holy Spirit opportunity, He will use that language to pray for your calling, to pray out the plan of God, to edify you, and to charge you with His holy power. He will lend Himself to you as your faith allows Him to be activated within your spirit. He will pull you *out of* everything Jesus set you free from and *into* everything Jesus says that you are still in Him (12).

Indeed, the purpose of the Holy Spirit is delineated in 1 Corinthians 2:9-14 where it states,

But, it is written, 'What no eye has seen, nor ear heard, nor the heart of man imagined, what God has prepared for those who love him' – these things God has revealed to us through the Spirit. For the Spirit searches everything even the depths of God. For who knows a person's thoughts except the spirit of that person, which is in him? So also no one comprehends the thoughts of God except the Spirit of God. Now we have received not the spirit of the world, but the Spirit who is from God, that we might understand the things freely given us by God. *And we impart this in words not taught by human wisdom but taught by the Spirit, interpreting spiritual truths to those who are spiritual* (my emphasis).

The impartation of spiritual truth takes place between man and God through the Holy Spirit who communicates the truth. He is the Speaker. We, in turn, are to use this knowledge given to us by the Holy Spirit to speak to others in prophesy, tongues and interpretation of tongues as prompted by the Spirit (Iverson). Roberson continues in his exposition of the Holy Spirit in the following:

My spirit is the part of me that is created in God's image, it is the candle of God. In other words, it is the part of me that the Holy Spirit ignites my understanding of Himself, imparting unto me revelation understanding....The Holy Spirit teaches us everything we cannot discern. He shows us mysteries and divine secrets we need to know about God and His ways. He is our first and foremost Teacher (178).

It can be surmised that the Holy Spirit provides divine discourse as the Communicator, the Great Teacher and Speaker.

Prayer language being the language that God the Spirit speaks on behalf of us can conversely be thought of as a faith language when it applies to the believer. The language reflects the faith of the believer, hence faith language. An example of faith language is found in the account recorded in Scripture of the Roman centurion who summoned Jesus to heal his servant.

> And Jesus went to them. When he was not far from the house, the centurion sent friends, saying to him, *'Lord, do not trouble yourself, for I am not worthy to have you under my roof. Therefore I did not presume to come to you. But say the word, and let my servant be healed. For I too am a man set under authority,*

with soldiers under me; and I say to one, 'Go,' and he goes, and to another, 'Come,' and he comes; and to my servant, 'Do this,' and he does it.' When Jesus heard these things, he marveled at him, and turning to the crowd that followed him, said, 'I tell you, not even in Israel have I found such faith (Luke 7:6-9, my emphasis).

Pastor Jack Hayford writes in his book, *Living the Spirit Formed Life,* about prayer being a combination of worship, fellowship, and intercession as the communication between man and God. Faith language spoken by believers also expresses itself in a mixture of worship, fellowship and intercession. Hayford describes prayer as the following but it can also be applied to indicate faith language. He writes, *"Worship* through adoration, praise and thanksgiving *to* God; *fellowship* through devotion, communion and conversation *with* God; *intercession* through supplication, fasting and spiritual warfare *before* God" (194).

Analysis of the centurion's words would reveal the properties of worship, fellowship and intercession in his faith language. Worship through adoration is seen in the centurion's address of Jesus as Lord and as One who is so magnificent that his house was not worthy for the Lord to even step foot in it.

Fellowship is demonstrated in the commonality that is shared as being under an authority; Jesus with God the Father and the centurion under Caesar. But because of the bond that they both share with a higher authority, the centurion recognizes the authority in Christ. He identifies it and submits himself to God the Son. In doing so, the centurion demonstrates humbleness, devotion and adoration of his Lord.

Reaching out to the Lord for the healing of his servant reveals the centurion's willingness to intercede on the servant's behalf. He did not have to do this for it was only a servant's life at stake, a life deemed of less value than a master's. But the intercession of the centurion showed love that he held for others who are disadvantaged.

Additionally, the centurion exemplified extraordinary faith by stating that Jesus' spoken word is all that is needed for the healing of his servant. Jesus was astonished of all that took place. He understood and confirmed the centurion's faith language by stating, "I tell you, not even in Israel have I found such faith."

The Lord was surprised at the words spoken by the centurion who was not an Israelite but a Gentile. The faith language spoken by the centurion apparently touched the Lord. It demonstrates that anyone can speak the faith language if one believes.

Summary

God has been established as the Author of language which is given to man as a gift. The original purpose of language was to glorify God. But as was demonstrated man had other plans. Nevertheless, language is shown as a manifestation through the triune God. God the Father as the source of meaning which takes on the fullness of God and through language transcends time and space. Doing so, language circumvents the intrusion of generational and sociological variances as well as time. Meaning perceived on this transcendal plane unyokes language from any and all humanistic interpretations. Hence, man is freed to find his being and worth in God's divine realm.

God as Son provides unity. Language is the medium that serves to unite man under God the Son. At one time, man was united and were of one accord but sinful man figured out how to use language to rebel against God. As a consequence God dispersed man by confusing the language (Genesis. 11:1-9). Today, there are a plethora of languages spoken but the meaning of words remain stable as long as people are grounded in the Word of God. The Word of God, that is, His Son who unites all. When He returns again, there will be only one language spoken, the original one that glorifies Him.

God the Spirit is the Speaker. The indwelling Holy Spirit is the One who reveals the will of the Lord to us in language the one can understand. Through this language He also instructs, convicts, guides and prays. But this is not a one way street of communication. There is also faith language that believers speak when they commune with the Lord. The language reflects three aspects. They are, worship through praise, exultation and thanksgiving to the Lord; fellowship through dedication, communion and discourse with the Lord and intercession through petition, fasting and spiritual warfare before the Lord.

Through the Holy Spirit, impartation of wisdom which is not known to man takes place. We are then charged to pass it on to the next generation. But, herein lies the problem. In order to teach others, the listener must understand the language spoken.

II.   MAN'S WORD VERSUS GOD'S WORD

Man's struggle since his fall continues to be a life separate from God. As was shown in Genesis 11:1-9, man's perceived weapon to unify all in order to rebel against God was in the use of language. After God confounded language causing much confusion, man continues to study the use of language in order to make a name for himself (Genesis 11:4). Traditionally the study of language involved the communication of ideas to one another through signs.

Semiotics is a contemporary branch of science that studies communication through signs. Its roots trace back to Plato (428-348 B.C.) and Aristotle (384-322 B.C.). Basically, semiotic studies focuses on the hegemony of natural signs which are those signs noted in natural creation and conventional signs that are used for communication (Cobley and Jansz). An example of how both signs interplay can be explained in a scenario where a person seeks medical help. The person will communicate the symptoms to the health practitioner. Based on the physical signs, diagnostics, laboratory data, health history of the person and the knowledge of the practitioner, a diagnosis is determined.

Current semiotics was developed by Ferdinand de Saussure (1857-1913), whose linguistic study was directed by the premise that "the process of communication through language involves the transfer of the contents of minds: the signs which make up the **code** of the circuit between the contents of the brain of each" (Cobley and Jansz 12). The process is the "code… carried out via the relationship (which is completely arbitrary) between the signifier (the speaker) and the signified (the hearer). The final end result is revealed in the linguistic sign that emerges" (Cobley and Jansz 12).

Another area in linguistic studies is viewed through a metaphysical lens ascertaining that language is a reflection of one's soul. The 20th century marked a turn in the study of language. A transformation of inquiry shifted from a philosophy of language to linguistic science. A review of philosophers and scientists in both areas of inquiry reveal an astonishing array of perspectives.

For each perspective given, there is another that counters it. For the purposes of lending some order to the vast field of language philosophy and linguistic science, three approaches to the nature of language will be presented and their prominent proponents. Through this presentation, the hope is that an understanding is garnered what man desires to accomplish through language.

Three approaches to the nature of language are divided into:

1. Private language where the viewpoint of John Locke (1634-1704), Ludwig Wittenstein (1889-1951) and Saul Kripke (1940) are presented.

2. A formal system of social phenomenon by David Lewis (1941-2001)

3. Language as an organ proposed by Noam Chomsky (1928) (Martinich).

Private Language

Locke was a British philosopher who is best known for his stance on the separation of church and state. His literary works typically reflect an obstinate position against authority especially in authoritarian beliefs. Locke believed in one's own reasoning process to arrive at any truth (www.Stanford Encyclopedia of Philosophy accessed 3/19/14). Locke theorized that carrying out these beliefs constituted language as a private matter. Although he does not explicitly state it as such, Locke maintains that the significance of all words are ideas.

For that matter then, words can only be relevant to the speaker only (as opposed to the listener too). The premise though, opens up a vast array of counterpoints. But Locke is undeterred in his position that although words can mean no more than ideas in one's mind, there are two understandings which is referred to as "secret reference". The first understanding is that the words articulated must be sounds that are familiar to others too (Locke in Martinich). Secondly, Locke continues with discourse of man as not only entailing the process of their own ideas but the words must convey some sort of reality (Locke in Martinich).

Locke's insight paved the way for further inquiry by Ludwig Wittenstein. The philosophical argument on the inherent nature of language continues with Wittenstein. He was a 20th century philosopher who had profound influence in the area of analytic philosophy (study of logic and mathematics and its influence on language). Wittenstein's tenets have impacted and continue to effect the areas of logic and thought, religion, ethics, authority and culture, perception and language (Stanford Encyclopedia of Philosphy).

In his philosophical premise of language, Wittenstein presents a contradiction. Initially Wittenstein proposed that private language is defined as words that are meaningful to the individual speaker only according to his/her perception (Martinich). He later offers a system of rules that need to be in play for such language to exist or to have meaning.

Is Wittenstein alluding to meaning as a phenomenon that is socially constructed by the community or the individual's perspective or sense of reality? If private language is an individual construct, then its fulcrum must be derived from a public language from whence it derives meaning. All in all, the glaring theme in the inquiry of "private language" is the source of meaning. Wittenstein contends that even "no action of action could be determined by a rule, because every course of action can be made to accord with the rule" (Kripke in Martinich). But where is the source of these rules? Do rules create meaning, which is then mirrored in language? The argument of private language is taken up by Saul Kripke as an opportunity to explore a way to reach genuine meaning.

Saul Kripke is an American philosopher whose work has contributed in the areas of logic, mathematics, metaphysics, epistemology and language. He is currently professor emeritus at Princeton University (www.princeton.edu accessed 4/2/14). Expounding on Wittenstein's philosophy of language, Kripke furthered the premise that meaning is derived from the community. Out of the seemingly contradictory stance of Wittenstein, Kripke addresses the issue of ideas (the personal) and present meaning. He proposes two polarizing but important interpretations that will set the course for further research. They are:

1. Language is essentially social.

2. Language is conceptually (even if not psychologically) possible that a lifelong Crusoe (e.i., a human being isolated from birth) should employ some kind of linguistic system and follow rules in so doing (Stanford Encyclopedia of Philosophy).

Language as a Formal System

David Lewis is an American philosopher and is the primary proponent of a language system that pairs sentences with a corresponding meaning. According to Lewis, meaning in a sentence is "something which, when combined with factual information about the world - or factual information about *any* possible world, yields a truth-value. It could therefore, be a function from worlds to truth-values- or more simply, a set of worlds" (Lewis in Martinich 656). For example, if X is part of Y language, then X could be a function of Y language. Therefore, X(Y) = meaning. Hence, X is true in the sentence of Y language in the world of Z if Z belongs in the world of X(Y). X as the operative in Y language can only be real or true if all possible worlds connect with X(Y) are true. (Lewis in Martinich). Such a process is known as semantics which is the study of the relation between language and the world (Martinich).

Lewis also states that the counter to the aforementioned logic is that language is also "a social phenomenon which is part of the natural history of human beings; a sphere of human actions, wherein people utter strings of vocal sounds, or inscribe strings of marks and where people respond by thought or action to the sounds or marks which they observe to have so produced" (656). The combination of semantics and social human behavior rests on the supposition of truth. But whose truth? For a certain community to adopt a particular language, to speak so everyone in the community can understand, there needs to be some sort of agreement. Lewis calls this "convention." Therefore, for anyone to adopt a language, the convention of veracity or "truthfulness" is perceived in the language. In the "perfect" world, both speaker and listener cooperate whereby when the speaker communicates, he/she believe he/she is speaking truth.

Whereas the hearer responds to the communication in truth and considers as he/she considers his/her beliefs. This interaction in the particular language continues because of each participant's past experience in its truthfulness. With each exchange, the idea of conformity takes hold whereby the speaker may want to pass on some belief. (Lewis in Martinich).

Lewis claims that language is not only based on the supposition of truth but also on "grammar." "A grammar according to Lewis, is a lexicon (e.i. a set of elementary constituents, along with their interpretation), a generative component (e.i. rules for combining constituents into larger constituents) and a representing component (e.i. rules for verbally expressing constituents" (Stanford Encyclopedia of Philosophy). The concept of grammars will be discussed later in detail but suffice to say for now that the notion of grammars of language allow for a plethora of language theories.

Language as an Organ

On April 28, 1986 Noam Chomsky, an American philosopher and generally known as the father of linguistics, a social activist and anarchist, delivered a paper at a conference in Madrid entitled, "Language and the Problem of Knowledge" (Chomsky in Martinich). In it, Chomsky set out to prove that up till then the philosophical tenets of language and its acquisition were pointless. They were pointless because they did not lead to a body of knowledge in linguistics. Chomsky begins by asking the question, "What do you mean by 'language?'" The present mindset is based on, according to Chomsky, intuitive commonsense concepts that operate on what is described as one's ability. "If one is to ask how a child acquires language and how a foreigner learns language, the answer would be that they both are 'on the way' towards acquisition" (Chomsky in Martinich 675).

Chomsky posits "if all adults were to die from sudden disease, and children of five or under were to survive, whatever it is that they were speaking would become a typical human language, though one that we say does not exist. Ordinary usage breaks down at this point, not surprisingly; its concepts are not designed from inquiry into the nature of language" (Chomsky in Martinich 675). The other contention is the pronunciation of words and the various dialects. The question is whether the pronunciation is right or wrong. All these issues, according to Chomsky, do not amount to any solid study of language, the mind and its complexities. Chomsky resoundingly refused the commonly held belief that language is a process of learning and is in favor of language grows in the mind/brain. To that end, Chomsky proposes, that at some remote period of evolutionary history, the brain developed a certain capacity for digital computation, for employing recursive rules and associated mental representations, thus acquiring the basis for thought and language in the human sense, with the arithmetical capacity perhaps latent as a kind of abstraction from the language faculty [the part of the brain that is dedicated to the acquisition of language including the production and understanding of sounds], to be evoked when cultural conditions allowed, much later, in fact never in the case of some societies, so it appears (Chomsky in Martinich 683).

In regards to the multitude of languages spoken around the world, Chomsky addresses it by stating that the underlying principles governing the spoken languages are the essential elements found in the language faculty of the brain. They are the same in all human brain/mind. He labels them as the Universal Grammar. The language faculty in the human brain is the crux of Chomsky's study of linguistics. The language faculty of the brain set humans apart from animals as being "species specific" (Chomsky). To that effect, Chomsky notes,

> the faculty of language can reasonably be regarded as a 'language organ' in the sense in which scientists speak of the visceral system as organs of the body. Understood in this way, an organ is not something that can be removed from the body, leaving the rest intact. It is a subsystem of a more complex structure. We hope to understand the full complexity of investigating parts that have distinctive characteristics, and through interactions. Study of the faculty of language proceeds in the same way (Martinich 4).

Placing language out of the philosophical realm into a natural one opens up the door to what Chomsky hopes to achieve. The goal would be the opportunity to develop "intelligent" (explanatory) theories and proving them as truth, thereby adding to the body of natural sciences. Indeed, some experimental studies conducted on a person named Christopher demonstrated some theoretical propositions. Christopher is believed to have an intact language faculty as evidenced by his ability to grasp sixteen languages and translate them into English. But Christopher also severely lacks cognitive skills. In the experiment, Christopher and a control group were used. Both learned Berber language and a fictitious system that disregards established principles of language. Christopher easily acquired the Berber language but was unable to do anything with the invented system of language principles because of his severe cognitive handicap.

The control group also was taught Berber and was able to make some headway with the fabricated principles of language. In the end, the conclusion made for the fabricated principles of language was that it was a puzzle (Chomsky 121). The point of the experiment was to demonstrate how the language organ of the brain exists with no connection to any properties of other cognitive processes.

Previously in the chapter, the term, grammar was introduced. The concept is vital in the study of linguistics. According to this concept, grammars arise by the interplay of the I – language which is the internal make-up or genetic structure of a person. The second aspect of grammar is the E – language which denotes symbols or signs. Chomsky is nebulous whether there is such a phenomenon as E - language. Nevertheless, the contention is that a particular grammar of an individual brain/mind is elicited by the effects of an experience. As such, Chomskian linguistic theory dictates that between the Universal Grammar found in the language faculty of the brain and the individual grammar best determines a solid and reliable perspective of language.

Up till the arrival of Chomsky, language was explained using a philosophical approach. Chomsky instead, chose the evolutionary scientific route explaining that language is a genetic issue. Man is endowed with a language faculty in the brain that developed a grammar which is an inherent database of language principles that are universal in all human beings. He believes that the language faculty evolved not so much by natural selection but with other processes in motion.

Future Scientific Studies

Doubting scientists find fault with Chomsky's theory and therefore propose another one. Still following Darwinian belief, the hypothesis put forth is that language is an organ much like other organs that comprise the human body. The way language has evolved is through generations of people speaking and listening under evolutionary processes of human learning. The progression of human learning and the processes of internalization has molded the brain and in turn language (Christiansen and Chester). Therefore, if language is shaped by the brain, the study of the brain organ with all its complexities would lead one into the world of language with all its variances. This endeavor could be aided with current sophisticated technology such as functional brain imaging modalities (Brown and Hagroot). The modality primarily used is magnetic resonance imaging (fMRI). Brain function as an organ is visualized by following oxygenated and deoxygenated blood supply to brain neurons during activity. This tracking of brain function can lead to the establishment of patterns in neural activity (Rugg in Brown and Hagoort).

Positron emission tomography (PET) affords a three dimensional representation of the body through pinpointing and measurement of radiation emissions. PET use is helpful in distinguishing neural activity in cognition. An enterprise as this requires two sets of imaging for comparison in order to arrive to a conclusion. For example, word seen versus word spoken (Rugg in Brown and Hagoort).

Another methodology employed to study language and the brain is the electroencephalogram (ECG). It measures neural electroactivity of the brain. In junction with its magnetic counterpart, (magnetic encephalogram or MEG) an event or specific time occurrence is measured (Rugg in Brown and Hagoort). The general consensus in language and mind/brain research is that there are many intricate processes that operate to coordinate, integrate sound, grammar and meaning among others in a split second time (Brown and Hagroot). What is not well established yet is the relationship of language in grammatical or its innateness and the brain organ. "Although neuroscience has by now learned a great deal about coarse brain localization of function, about the functioning of individual neurons and small collection of neurons, and about effects of neurotransmittors on brain processes, it cannot yet tell us much about the details of language" (Jackendoff in Brown and Hagoort 39). Scientists have claimed that they cannot go beyond into the specifics of language. Yet science continues to be the avenue through which man seeks to make a name for himself, a way to declare his word over God's.

At this point, it may very well be where the Lord allows man to proceed no further. He is the Author of language and will remain as such. Being the Creator of earth and all that exists in it, man should have a healthy curiosity about the wonders of God's creation. Science is a way to discover these wonders. It should be the avenue towards discovering the miracles of God. All glory and honor ought to go the One who conceives such things. Actually, the true propose of science and all its branches is to celebrate God. Sadly, man uses science to uncover and give the credit to anyone or anything other than God.

A case in point is Dr. Francis Collins, discoverer of the human genome, geneticist and former atheist. Outstanding in his field of science, he cracked the human genetic code. In doing so, Collins discovered something so wonderfully complex that he concluded that such marvel can only be created by the Almighty God. In his book entitled *The Language of God*, Collins writes,

> The comparison of chimp and human sequences [genetic patterns], interesting as it is, does not tell us what it means to be human. In my view, DNA sequence alone, even if accompanied by a vast trove of data on biological function, will never explain certain special human attributes, such as the knowledge of Moral Law and the universal search

for God. Freeing God from the burden of special acts of creation does not remove Him as the source of the things that make humanity special, and of the universe itself. It merely shows us something of how He operates (140-141).

Indeed, God's creation is a revelation of Himself.

God's Word

God's word is straight forward. His word is the final say in all matters. It is bared "day to day [as it] pours out speech, and night to night reveals knowledge. There is no speech, nor are there words, whose voice is not heard. Their voice goes out through all the earth, and their words to the end of the world" (Ps. 19:2-4). The Old Testament testifies of God's timing and events that led to the coming of His Son. God used words, His language, to communicate with people using the mouths of His chosen prophets.

In the prophet Moses, God tells him to go and announce to the Israelites that God, the God of their fathers appeared to him. The Lord said, "And they will listen to your voice, and you and the elders of Israel shall go to the king of Egypt and say to him, 'The Lord, the God of the Hebrews, has met with us; and now, please let us go a three day journey into the wilderness, that we may sacrifice to the Lord our God'" (Genesis 4: 18-20). Note the authority of God's words, "they will listen to your voice."

When God called the prophet Jeremiah, Jeremiah was concerned. He responded to God by saying, "Ah, Lord God! Behold I do not know how to speak, for I am only a youth." But the Lord said to [him], "Do not say, 'I am only a youth; for to all whom I send you, you shall go, and whatever I command you, you shall speak. Do not be afraid of them, for I am with you to deliver you,' declares the Lord" (Jeremiah 1:6-8). Jeremiah's attitude towards God was not one who was seeking excuses not to serve Him.

As a youth, he was still under his parent's authority. God assures Jeremiah that all is well as the Higher Authority who will give him the words to speak. He was not to fear for the Lord would be with him just as a parent would guide and protect his/her child.

Even the contentious prophet Balaam knew that he was under obligation to speak the words of God above his own. "Balaam said to Balak, 'Behold, I have come to you! Have I now any power of my own to speak anything? The words that God puts in my mouth that I must speak'" (Numbers 22:38). "And Balak said to Balaam, 'What have you done to me? I took you to curse my enemies and behold, you have done nothing, but bless them.' And he answered and said, 'Must I not take care to speak what the Lord puts in my mouth?'" (Numbers 23:11-12).

Balaam was quite aware of the power the God of the Israelites possessed. He knew that the nation of Israel escaped slavery in Egypt because their God spoke and it came to be. Balaam tried to curse them and instead he spoke blessings. Therefore, Balaam had a healthy fear of the Lord. "The fear of the Lord is the beginning of wisdom; all those who practice it have a good understanding (Psalm 111:10). For those who love the Lord, He will use the mouth for His glory. "Now therefore go and I will be with your mouth and teach you what you shall speak" (Exodus 4:12).

After the resurrection, Jesus says to His disciples,

These are my words that I spoke to you while I was still with you, that everything written about me in the Law of Moses and the Prophets and the Psalms must be fulfilled.' Then he opened their minds to understand the Scriptures and said to them, 'Thus it is written that the Christ should suffer and on the third day rise from the dead, and that repentance and forgiveness of sins should be proclaimed in his name to all nations, beginning in Jerusalem. You are witnesses of these things. And behold, I am sending the promise of my Father to you' (Luke 24:44-49).

The day of Pentecost signaled the coming of the Holy Spirit, the power from on high that Jesus promised to all who loved Him. In 2 Peter, Paul conveyed his sense of certainty in the power of the Lord's words through the Holy Spirit. He writes,

> And we have something more sure, the prophetic word, to which you will do well to pay attention as to a lamp shining in a dark place, until the day dawns and the morning star rises in your hearts, knowing this first of all, that no prophecy of Scripture comes from someone's interpretation. For no prophecy was ever produced by the will of man, but men spoke from God as they were carried along by the Holy Spirit (1:19-21).

To that end, the assurance of truth is anchored in Scripture, His word.

Just as bold and authoritative Paul was with the confidence as promised in Exodus 4:12, man is commanded to do the same without compromising. To compromise His word would compromise truth. For what was foretold by the prophets of the Old Testament has been fulfilled in Jesus Christ "restoring all the things about which God spoke" (Acts 3:22).

The word of God is established as the voice of authority and truth. Therefore, His word is absolute. The book of Revelation, declares that Jesus will come again on judgment day. He describes Himself in the book as, "'The Alpha and the Omega'... 'who is and who was and who is to come, the Almighty'" (1:8). In the meantime, we are reminded through the book of Jude to recall "the predictions of the apostles of our Lord Jesus Christ. They said to you, 'In the last time there will be scoffers, following their ungodly passions.' It is these who cause division, worldly people devoid of the Spirit. But you, beloved, building yourselves up in your most holy faith and praying in the Holy Spirit, keeping yourselves in the love of God waiting for the mercy of our Lord Jesus Christ that leads to eternal life" (17-21).

Watchman Nee was a 20th century Chinese Christian convert and missionary. In 1952, the Chinese government imprisoned him for his faith. He died there in 1972. His book entitled *The Breaking of the Outer Man and the Release of the Spirit*, explains how the will of man of his flesh is contrary to the spoken word of God. Watchman gives a detailed account of what it takes to crucify the outer man. He states that for some people it may takes years for this to happen and for others it may never occur. This may be due to a strong will, a passionate sentiment, ("a stubborn heart," Ezekiel 2:7)), and a tough mind ("hard forehead," Ezekiel 2:7).

Watchman continues with the reasons why people will not submit to the work of the Lord. First, they live in darkness. He describes it as not able to "see" God's hand. God is working and breaking, yet they do not know that God is doing the work. They only see men, thinking that men are opposing them. Or they only see the immediate surroundings, complaining that it is too harsh and placing blame on the environment. Does this not resemble what present day society labels as "victimization?"

The second reason is the promotion of self-love. "Because we love ourselves secretly, we try to save ourselves. This is a big problem. Many times problems arise because we try to save ourselves" (13). Furthermore,

Watchman notes that God has placed a spirit within each one of us that will act in response to the Lord. However, this spirit will only react to external signals (23). One of these signals is language. The language of the spoken Gospel functions to open the door of the person's spirit. In order to do that, testifying Christians must know the language of the other.

Summary

Regardless of the authoritative voice and truth of the Lord, man continues to rebel against His Word. A very brief outline of man's attempts to dispute the word of God is presented from a philosophical stance to present day scientific endeavors. Technological advances in scientific diagnostics hope to reclassify language as a gift of God that glorifies Him to a human body organ. A major and influential proponent is Noam Chomsky. Advances in linguistic and neurocognitive studies seem to support the "organ" theory. The underpinnings involve evolution and "species – specific" concepts. Much is yet unexplained because many questions still remain unanswered.

This may very well be where God allows no more probing in linguistics, maintaining His precious gift of language. The absolute, powerful and truthful words of God are spoken "for no prophecy was ever produced by the will of man, but men spoke from God as they were carried along by the Holy Spirit" (2 Peter1:21). "God our Savior … desires all people to be saved and to come to the knowledge of truth" (1 Timothy 2:3-4). "Therefore go and [God] will be with your mouth and teach you what you shall speak" (Exodus 4:12).

III.   CONTEXTUALIZATION

Contextualization is a tool used in the toolbox of hermeneutics whereby Scripture is considered in its original or intended meaning. In Bible exegesis, contextualization perceives the historical – cultural backdrop of Scripture. Then it determines how to bring it forward, finding the specific words that will convey the intended meaning to current cultures. Contextualization forms the bridge that connects the world of yesterday with today (Klein, Blomberg, and Hubbard, Jr.).

It has been practiced since the 1960's during a tumultuous time in the United States history as a response to the decade's perceived narrowed sensitivity to particular societal groups. By the early 1970's, the term came in vogue as Christianity strove to acknowledge cultural aspects such as language and tradition in order to better serve the populace. Such movement, though, provided the platform for present liberation theology in South American, African and Asian third world countries.

A social gospel was birthed that also incorporated economic, political as well as language and cultural aspects of the society. The occurrence of the Social Gospel in the 1970's demonstrated how easily one can cross the line from being in the world to being of the world (Osso, *Synthesis*).

Jesus called His disciples to minister in His name in order to reach unbelievers. We are called to "be a vessel for honorable use, set apart as holy, useful to the Master of the house, ready for every good work" (2 Timothy 2:21). As far as contextualization is concerned, we are to follow the example of Paul as he preached the Gospel in various societies. In 1 Corinthians 9:19-23, he states,

> For though I am free from all, I have made myself a servant to all, that I might win more of them. To

the Jew, I became a Jew, in order to win Jews. To those under the law I became as one under the law (though not being myself under the law) that I might win those under the law. To those outside the law I became as one outside the law (not being outside the law of God but under the law of Christ) that I might win those outside the law. To the weak I became weak that I might win the weak. I have become all things to all people that by all means I might save some. I do it all for the sake of the gospel, that I may share with them in its blessings.

How is the example of Paul actualized today? Dr. Nelson Jennings, a former missionary answers the question in an article entitled, "Looking Forward: Voices from Church Leaders on Our Global Mission." He writes,

Consider Christianity's basic trait of cultural and contextual *translatability*. God as Creator is wholly separate from His creation: He is transcendent. Yet God has remained involved with His fallen creation, preeminently through entering the world as a concrete man, becoming particularized, or contextualized as Jesus of Nazareth. At the same time, God's Word, which centers and focuses on Jesus, speaks to all people in their particular language as the Bible is (re) translated again and again into new (and changing) languages, Jesus comes close to all kinds of people, to every tribe, tongue, and nation. He is not a provincial or tribal Savior, but He is the covenant Lord and Redeemer of all the earth. Together with translated Word, Jesus crosses over cultural and generational boundaries and enters new contexts, shouldering His way into the beliefs of all kinds of people. Unlike Islam, for example, which brings into alien settings, and enduring Arabic Qur'an and foundations of life, Jesus and His Word are translated over new settings, whereby people come to worship and follow Him with the terms and contours of their own language and contexts.

Indeed the contextualization of Scripture not only refers to people living in different countries, it also pertains to our current society. The latest Barna research has shown a shift in meanings. As Christians reach out to non-believers or to the Christian poor in spirit, we try to identify with them. "We don't judge them for our Lord does not judge" (Richards 50).

Dr. Philip Gary Richards writes in his book entitled, *The Minister's Life of Obedience*, about the call for Christians to be preachers/teachers. He cites 1 Corinthians 19:22 as a model for such use; "a life of obedience and becoming all things to all men" (49). Richards also notes that in the King James translation of the Bible, to serve people for the sake of blessing them in the name of the Lord, we need to consider others and practices. He adds that in discerning the needs of others, ministers of God should be service tempered in dealing with others, careful not to cause resentment (51). A situation depicted in Bible helps to demonstrate this point. Upon his return to Antioch, Paul found Peter separated from the community to eat with only the Christian Jews. Paul writes the book of Galatians,

> But when Cephas [Peter] came to Antioch, I opposed him to his face, because he stood condemned. For before certain men came from James he was eating with the Gentiles, but when they came he drew back and separated himself, fearing the circumcision party. And the rest of the Jews acted hypocritically along with him, so that even Barnabas was led astray by their hypocrisy. But when I saw that their conduct was not in step with the truth of the gospel, I said to Cephas [Peter] before them all, 'If you, though Jew, live like a Gentile and not like a Jew, how can you force the Gentiles to live like a Jew?" (2:11-14).

For all saints, the passage portrays walking the tightrope of relevance. Will it be as the Reformed brethren say, "Sola Scripture?" Will the lingo change to "sola cultura" in order to be relevant to the prevailing culture (Wells)? Relevance to a postmodern society places emphasis on feelings and affections over against linear thought and rationality; on experience over against truth; on inclusion over against exclusion; on participation over against individualism and the heroic loner. For some, this means a move from the absolute to the authentic. It means taking into account contemporary emphasis on tolerance, it means not telling others they are wrong (Carson 29).

Presently, relevance and contextualization are being meshed as one with contextualization taking on the mantra of "sola cultura" in its zeal to reach others with the Good News. A new movement within the mission field is gaining traction both in the Reformed and Evangelical spheres of Christianity and causing alarm. I would describe it more of a sensibility that is rapidly turning missiology on its head. The new sensibility is called the Insider Movement.

Missiology

Jesus bridged the Old and New Testaments. Christians must bridge Scripture, the infallible word of God, to the lost. Whether liberal or conservative in thought, knowledge of language as well as values and symbols of a society or generation are pre-requisites before embarking on a journey to spread the Good News. Missiology is a buzz word in the realm of theology that is increasingly talked about. Missiology is defined as "getting to know a person and his or her culture in turn, the gospel can be contextualized to that person or people groups." (Driscoll 143).

This does not mean that Christians need to adopt cultural aspects that may be in conflict with the word of God in order to reach the people. A Christian must live a life according to the word of God without succumbing to societal traditions and customs that are not in line with Christianity. We are called to be set apart, holy unto the Lord.

In the book, *The Supremacy of Christ in a Postmodern World*, Dr. Tim Keller writes that contextualization is, showing people how the lines of their own lives, the hopes of their own hearts, and the struggles of their own cultures will be resolved in Jesus Christ. David Wells says that contextualization requires, 'not merely a practical application of biblical doctrine but a translation of that doctrine into a conceptuality that meshes with the reality of the social structures and patterns of life dominant in our contemporary life...Where is the line between involvement and disengagement, acceptance and denial, continuity and discontinuity, being 'in' the world and not 'of' the world?

Contextualization is the process through which we find answer to these questions. The Word of God must be related to our own context... The preservation of its identity is necessary for Christian belief; its contemporary relevance is required if Christians are to be believable (117-118).

Missiology is pursuing the fulfillment of the Great Commission by Jesus Christ. "And Jesus came and said to them, 'All authority in heaven and on earth has been given to me. Go therefore, and make disciples for all nations, baptizing them in the name of the Father and of the Son and of the Holy Spirit, teaching them to observe all that I have commanded you. And behold, I am with you always, to the end of the age" (Matthew 28: 18-29). Jesus is the foremost model in the missionary field; He ministers but never compromises. He is the first person who was able to successfully contextualize His Father's words to a society who had another perspective.

Using what He had at His disposal, Jesus worked to help people understand through His behavior, parables, miracle and healings. He was kind and patient as He shed light on the truth. At other times He became incensed at the hypocrisy of man, especially the religious leaders of the day. An example is found in Matthew 15:3-9. Jesus answered the Pharisees and scribes,

> And why do you break the commandment of God for the sake of your tradition? For God commanded, 'Honor your father and your mother' and 'Whoever reviles father and mother must surely die. But you say, 'If anyone tells his father or mother,' What you would have gained from me is given to God,' he need not honor his father for the sake of your tradition you have made void the word

of God. You hypocrites! Will did Isaiah prophesy to you, when he said, 'This people honors me with their lips, but their heart is far from me; in vain do they worship me, teaching as doctrines the commandments of man'

The Pharisees and scribes were offended, but Jesus stood firm on His Father's word. He did not compromise by yielding to the prevailing culture and traditions.

Consider the parable of the sower, the first one shared by Jesus. Matthew 13:3-8 records the following words of Jesus.

A sower went out to sow. And as he sowed, some seeds fell along the path, and the birds came and devoured them. Other seeds fell on rocky ground, where they did not have much soil, immediately they sprang up, since they had no depth of soil, but when the sun rose they were scorched. And since they had no root, they withered away. Other seeds fell on good soil and produced grain, some a hundredfold, some sixty, some thirty.

The missionary is the sower. Before he/she sows the seeds of the Good News, the missionary must survey the "soil" that the seeds would be planted in as well as the environment. The environmental surveillance would look for conditions that foster or deter the growth of the seed. Watering of the seed is essential for growth and maturation. The water would be the language the missionary speaks. Language is important because "faith comes from hearing and hearing comes through the word of Christ" (Romans 10:17).

In consultation with Scripture, there are basically three simple steps to missiology. They are;

1. Follow His directives. Matthew 10:5-6 states "These twelve Jesus sent out, instructing them, 'Go nowhere among the Gentiles and enter no town of the Samaritans, but go rather to the lost sheep of the house of Israel.'" Jesus issued very specific instructions to His apostles that entail spreading the Gospel to the Jews first. Later on, mission work was extended to the Gentiles and throughout the world.

The apostles were being trained to <u>follow only His directives</u> as opposed to any notion of missiology of their own. These instructions may have sounded strange to the apostles but it made them aware of their dependence on their Master.

2. Use the gifts of the Spirit as God wills. "And proclaim as you go, saying, 'The kingdom of heaven is at hand. Heal the sick, raise the dead, cleanse the leper, cast out demons. You received without pay; give without pay'" (Matthew 10:7-8). The gifts of the Holy Spirit such as healing whether physically or spiritually or casting out evil spirits for the purpose of cleansing still exist today. These gifts will continue to work as long as they are used in God's timing until Jesus returns again. "For we know in part and we prophesy in part, but when the perfect comes, the partial will pass away" (1 Corinthians 14:9). Eternal life was bought with the blood of Jesus as a propitiation of man's sin. Since it is received without paying, mission work must give without recompense. Mirror Jesus and the gifts

will manifest as His will is sought. Called to speak His word, we entrust ourselves in His will confirming His message by using His gifts. The message becomes an event. It becomes alive, tangible so people can perceive. God's language is actualized. No human language can wield such power.

3. He provides. "Acquire no gold nor silver nor copper for your belts, nor bag nor your journey, nor two tunics not sandals nor a staff, for the laborers deserves his food." (Matthew 10: 9-10). Jesus strips his apostles of money, valuables and anything of comfort or support. The message here is we don't need anything to achieve His call for the mission. He will provide all the essentials that are needed. Suddenly there is a lightness, the mission is no longer perceived as a great load. On the contrary, there is freedom and reward to do the work of God.

The Gospels were originally addressed to specific audiences. The book of Matthew was written with the

Jews in mind. The book of Mark was for the Romans and the book of Luke for the Gentiles. The book of John was written for the Greeks. There is much to be learned how these books were written, contextualizing the gospel for each group of people. Those lessons are becoming less significant today as culture is becoming more instrumental in defining God's message. Missiology has morphed and the change is fueled by the Insider Movement.

Inside the Insiders Movement

The 21st century marks a rejection of Western philosophy and logic. The adherence to traditional Christian principles has produced a backlash. Where the goal for Christianity is for unity in Christ while celebrating diversity, the postmodern mindset espouses otherwise.

Such a mindset proclaims that for Christianity to be relevant, it must take on the identity of societal culture. Therefore, for the modern missionary to extend the Good News to as many people as possible, the socio-religious must be considered as well as the socio-economic, political, morals, linguistic and philosophical aspects of the particular people.

Altruistic indeed, but this premise poses a certain danger depending on the degree of cultural accommodation. Christ's Great Commission is to spread the Good News without compromising the truth that is inherent in the message. The message flows from God through the missionary who speaks the words to the listening group. Proponents of the Insider Movement (IM) adjust the Word of God to fit a specific societal group, compromising the gospel. An example how Scripture is used for the purposes of IM is found in 1 Corinthians 9:19-23. It states,

> For though I am free from all, I have made myself a servant to all, that I might win more of them. To the Jews I became as a Jew, in order to win Jews. To those under the law I became as one under the law (though not being myself under the law) that I might win those under the law. To those outside

the law I became as one outside the law (not being outside the law of God but under the law of Christ) that I might win those outside the law. To the weak I became weak, that I might win the weak. I have become all things to all people that by all means I might save some. I do it all for the sake of the gospel that I may share with them in its blessings.

Many denominations, including evangelicals are jumping on this bandwagon. Why? Because on the surface, IM appears to be in keeping with Scripture and considered benign. Though, at its core is the central dispute when is a person converted to Christianity? Proponents of IM reject this argument.

As previously explained, language and meaning serve to unite believers under God and this is accomplished through the life and work of Jesus Christ. Therefore, all share citizenship in the Kingdom of God. The Kingdom of God is also a society or community with its own culture, language, morals and structure.

Pastor Philip Mark, missionary in the Muslim community writes in an article for "Reformation 21" on June 12, 2014, an online site for Reformed theology, the following,

A Christian has a singular ultimate identity, which is in Christ. An individual identity derived from the corporate – in being baptized into Christ's body is a spiritual identity...Spiritual identity refers to the ultimate, holistic and comprehensive identity wrought by the Holy Spirit. It is a 'reality on the ground' embedded in the concrete historic event and resurrection with Christ to newness of life. This identity that can be studied by the sciences but cannot be fully comprehended by them because it is resident in the age to come. It is an identity which is exhaustively defined in the nature of its relationship to God. The Christian is a covenant-keeper in Christ which is in utter and complete contrast to the prior identity of covenant-breaker in Adam.

The purity and holiness in a relationship with God and promised in Scripture is deconstructed by the IM supporters. The ability to deconstruct the Word of God is due to the Bible not considered inerrant. Promulgated by the Fuller Seminar Theological Seminary, the campus think-tank has unleashed a new experiment in the way to do mission work. Combining the sciences of anthropology and sociology with scripture, IM was birthed.

To the adherents of IM, the interpretation of this passage would necessitate the embracement of Muslim, Hindu, Buddhist, Wiccan and any other non- Christian community's customs and ideas. These groups can continue to attend their mosques and temples, keeping their worship rituals, practices and prayers. Allah, Buddha, Mohammed, Mother Earth and any other god is affirmed by Christians.

The Qur'an and all religious teachings and books are included as part of the societal identity and are to be accepted or at least tolerated. Paul stated in the passage that although he walked into these communities on his mission trips, he respected their rules but did not partake in them. As disciples of the Lord, the citizenship enjoyed in the Kingdom of God is not to be forsaken. As with any traveler going to a foreign country, observation of laws, rules and etiquette are observed. But the identity of the traveler is still maintained, as confirmed in the traveler's passport.

The passport is not checked in at the custom's booth upon entering the country. The same holds for Christian missionaries. The task is to bring the "word [as] a lamp to one's feet and a light to [one's] path" (Psalm 119:105). Jesus says,

> Whatever town or village you enter, find out who is worthy in it and stay there until you depart. As you enter the house, greet it. And if the house is worthy, let your peace come upon it, but if it is not worthy, let your peace return to you. And if anyone will not receive you or listen to your words, shake off the dust from your feet when you leave that house or town (Matthew 10:11-14).

What then, is the intended meaning of this passage for today? Pastor Mark gives an answer. He states,

> Christian society is governed by Christ and non-Christian society is governed by Satan. If any non-Christian society were to be consistent with its non-Christian beliefs, then the Christians would be killed. There is no toleration for light in darkness. However, God's common grace restrains evil and permits gospel witness to continue in varying degrees in different contexts. Due to this common grace, it is often the case that Christians are not killed and are rather permitted to live and be a witness. This, likewise is the case in Muslim society. Toleration, to the extent that it exists, as in any society, is obliged to live a life of integrity and faithful gospel witness, depending on God to watch over him or her and to bring fruit from this witness.

True the grace of God is what sustains and protects those who do the work of the Lord. It seems that the IM advocators have lost sight of this essential truth thinking that through relevance and tolerance there will be greater acceptance of the gospel. Jesus did not humble Himself to come into this world to compromise with the leaders of the day. "He himself bore our sins on his body on the tree, that we might die to sin and live to righteousness. By his wounds you have been healed.

For you were straying like sheep, but now returned the Shepherd and Overseer of your souls" (1 Peter 2:24-25). Jesus invites us to come out of the context of one's life of sin to enter a new context filled with righteousness. Through the atoning work of Jesus Christ, the bondage of sin is broken and true freedom is offered. "We know that our old self [the old context in life] was crucified in Him in order that the body of sin might be brought to nothing, so that we could no longer be enslaved by sin" (Romans 6:6).

True Contextualization

Every Christian has a responsibility to translate the Word of God to people so they can understand it. The standard should be contextualization of the Christian faith the way God would have it be. The IM proponents should ask themselves if God would really tolerate Allah alongside Him? How about Mohammed or Buddha on equal ground with Jesus? The commandment of the Lord, "You shall have no other gods before me" (Exodus 20:3) still holds today as it did during Moses' time.

The fact is that it is not about man but about Him! God was the first to use the concept of contextualization. He did it this way. "In the beginning was the Word, and the Word was God. All things were made through Him and without Him was not anything made that was made. In Him was life and the life was the light of man.

The light shines in the darkness, and the darkness has not overcome it…The true light, which enlightens everyone, was coming into the world" (John1:1-5,9). "And the Word became flesh and dwelt among us" (John 1:14). Jesus is described as a "light that shines in the darkness" of this world, a beacon that darkness [Satan] cannot overcome. The light brings with it truth and moral purity in the form of God incarnate. "For all who did receive Him, who believed in His name, He gave the right to become children of God, who were born, not of blood, nor of the will of the flesh, nor of the will of man, but of God" (John 1:12-13).

The contextualization of God into man through Jesus is now offered to mankind. Jesus offers man to leave the present life of sin and darkness and be reborn, start afresh as a child of God.

> Those who trust in Christ become caught up in this great work of God. Through faith we become united to Christ, joined to Him in such a way that His death becomes our death (we died in Him), and also so that His life becomes our life (we are raised in Him). God's work in us has the same shape as God's work in Christ. He gives us new resurrection life... With it we enjoy a whole host of newness: a new life, a new perspective and new ambition (Allberry 56).

The life and work of Jesus Chris lifts us from a context where,

> we were dead in the trespasses and sins in which [we] once walked following the course of the world, following the prince of air [Satan], the spirit that is now at work in the sons of disobedience- among whom we all once lived in the passions of our flesh, carrying out the desires of the body and the mind, and were by nature children of wrath, like the rest of mankind (Ephesians 2:1-3).

The process of contextualization that is specific to the work and plan of God is actualized in the process of sanctification. "At the very moment of our justification we become 'saints' for we have been 'sanctified in Christ Jesus' set apart to belong to the holy people of God (Acts 20:32, 1Corinthians 1:2, 6:11, Hebrews 10:29, 13:12). At other times, sanctification describes the process of growing in holiness and becoming Christ-like (Romans 6:19, 2 Corinthians 7:1, 1 Thessalonians 4:3, 5:2, Hebrews 12:14)"

(Stott 183). The Greek word for holiness is hagiosyne which means "sanctification, sanctity" (Mounce 789).

The setting apart of ourselves from the rest of the world and pursuing the process of becoming Christ-like, that is holy, puts us into another context. Spiritual contextualization takes place and this contextualization must be communicated to others. The crux of contextualization is what happens within. Bible exegesis is therefore, required to go beyond the ordinary way of hermeneutics to include the spirituality of contextualization. The Insider Movement and Missiology confirms that the usual way of contextualization opens the door to many interpretations of it.

Our Christian faith goes upward, vertically where our life is lived for the glory of God. Yes, our Christian faith extends horizontally as we reach out to our brethren and the world. But our primary focus is on the Lord. Therefore, contextualization, as it is defined today in Christianity is being applied incorrectly. The focus has to be reversed where instead of man being accommodated, man accommodates God. Dr. James Hamilton, Jr., author and professor at Southern Baptist Theological Seminary, says that a life transformed by the saving grace of the Lord is as follows. "Through His Word, written in the Bible, the Word becomes our metanarrative that forms our identity, creates our community, provides our shared foundation of language, builds our common network of assumption and dictates our response to international, local and personal events" (*God's Glory in Salvation Through Judgment. A Biblical Theology* 568). This is true contextualization.

Summary

Contextualization is a tool used in Bible exegesis to bring the intended meaning of Scripture forward to present day. The usual way of contextualization in hermeneutics is contested, revealing that in doing so, various interpretations of contextualization have erupted. Missiology and the Insider Movement are presented as examples of these interpretations. An alternative to modern interpretation of mission work, three steps based on Scripture are offered. The intention is to fulfill the commandment of Jesus Christ as He originally intended in Mathew 28: 16-20. They are,

1. Follow His directives.
2. Use the spiritual gifts that the Lord has given as He wills.
3. He provides.

The Insider Movement (IM) has helped to fuel the reinterpretation of mission and the contextualization of the gospel in the mission field. IM proponents maintain that to garner favor and eventual acceptance in the mission field, the socio-economic, political, moral, religious traditions and culture must be embraced. This would include whatever god or gods that the community worships. But is this what Jesus says constitutes a true rebirth?

Contextualization is more than what is purported by the IM proponents. There is also a spiritual aspect that takes place when one accepts Jesus Christ as his/her Lord. The saved one goes from the context of a dark and sinful life to one that is filled with joy, hope and a rebirth into eternal life and a totally different context. The whole context of being that is the way one lives, thinks and speaks emanate from this new context. The bridge from the context of sin and death to the context of eternal life is Jesus.

Missiology needs to embrace this concept of contextualization, not the context of the society that they are ministering to, in order to bring a true transformation in the individual. Contextualization is respecting the society being ministered to but never losing the context of Christianity.

VI.   DECONSTRUCTION

Deconstruction is a tool birthed upon the premise that absolute truth does not exist. Used by postmodernists, deconstruction encourages pluralism and relativity over objectivity and authority. As a consequence, all matters pertaining to truth are collapsed into a reality based on individualistic perspectives. Deconstruction is the instrument to achieve that end. Notoriously difficult to define, deconstruction is,

> an anarchistic, hyper-relativistic form of criticism
> designed to demonstrate how all texts, indeed all
> human communication ultimately deconstructs or
> undermines itself...Deconstruction normally seeks
> subtle, often unwitting ideological inconsistencies

or ambiguities in a text that seem hard to resolve and that prevents interpreters from claiming that it has a fixed meaning (Klein, Blomberg, Hubbard 75-76).

These inconsistencies, ambiguities are termed "differences," a term coined by Jacques Derrida (1930-2004).

Derrida was an atheist French philosopher who by the 1960's became influential in changing western philosophy. Up till then, philosophy about man and the world was categorized into neat systems known as structuralism. Derrida's claim is that to do so would assume a position of authority. The counter culture wave of the 1960's served to fan the flame of rebellion against any authoritarianism. By the late 1960's, poststructuralist philosophy emerged with Derrida at its helm (Osso, *Superficial Society, Synthesis*). The concepts of deconstruction and difference out of the poststructuralist philosophy are attributed to Derrida. According to him, the conventional notion of meaning "depends on an assumption of a 'metaphysics of presence,' that is, the full meaning of the word is held to be 'present' to the speaker or writers, in their mind as they use it" (Sims and Van Loon 88). Using Hegelian dialect, he asserts that there is always some meaning of its opposite, never an exclusive meaning (Osso, *Superficial Society, Synthesis*). From this point, Derrida takes on the task of deconstructing words in order to prove that there is no certainty in meaning.

Christianity has certainly felt its impact especially in hermeneutics. To that effect, critical theory is cited as the broad influence in postmodern paradigm of thinking and perception. Critical theory has been labeled as the theory of everything. Rooted in the philosophy of Georg Wilhelm Hegel, critical theory purports that nothing is certain. In order for anything (thesis) to have being, purpose, definition or meaning, it must turn to its opposite or antithesis.

A synthesis of both the thesis and antithesis takes place to create a new being, purpose, definition or meaning. In order to progress from there, the new entity must look to its antithesis and the whole process of synthesis repeats.

The objective of the process is to reach perfection. Critical theory revels in poststructuralist philosophy, thriving in postmodern society including Christian theology. Hence, the claim as the theory of everything. What critical theory strives to do above all is to negate truth. Translated in current postmodern society, relativity, pluralism, diversity and "tolerance" are celebrated.

The Effects of Deconstruction on Christianity

In the first letter to the Corinthians, Paul humbly writes, "And I, when I came to you, brothers, did not come proclaiming to you the testimony of God with lofty speech or wisdom...that your faith might not rest in the wisdom of man but in the power of God...And we impart this in words not taught by human wisdom but taught by the Spirit, interpreting spiritual truths to those who are spiritual" (2:1,5,13).

Paul continues in verse 14, "The natural person does not accept the things of the Spirit of God, for they are folly to him, and he is not able to understand them because they are spiritually discerned." Clearly, Paul teaches that the understanding of God's word can only be comprehended with the aid of the Holy Spirit. The words that Paul wrote and spoke to his audiences were through the power of the Holy Spirit.

Traditionally, Bible studies focus on Scripture and what God's message is in each verse. The meaning in the text are presumed to be fixed, respecting the Author's intended message. But of late, the reader-response criticism has taken hold in hermeneutics whereby the reader's reaction to the text is primary instead of the author's message. Therefore, meaning is not found in the author but in the reader's interpretation. Thus, for any given Bible passage that has a clearly stated meaning, the text can be read to mean many other ways.

An example of a reader-response critique is in the case of antinomianism. Antinomianism involves the interpretation of law in the Old Testament as it relates to the New Testament. The topic of law in the Bible has been subject of debate since the Reformation but today it seems to be more contentious. The concerns in the 17th century continue to echo today. They are:

1. To say we are justified by faith is an unsafe speech; we must say that we are justified by Christ.

2. To evidence justification by sanctification or graces savours of Rome. [Today there is Radical Orthodoxy and Ancient Future Theology taking up the mantle as well].

3. If I be holy, I am never the better accepted by God; if I be unholy, I am never the worse.

4. If Christ will let me sin, let him look to it; upon his honour be it.

5. Here is a great stir about graces and looking to hearts; but give me Christ; I seek not for graces, but for Christ...I seek not for sanctification, but for Christ; tell me not of meditation and duties, but tell me of Christ.

6. I may know I am Christ's, not because I do crucify the lust of my flesh, but because I do not

crucify them but believe in Christ that crucified my lusts for me.

7. If Christ be my sanctification, what need I look to anything in myself, to evidence my justification? (Jones 10-11)

Law never went away when Jesus came. He came "not to abolish law, but to fulfill them. For truly [Jesus] says to you, until heaven and earth pass away, not an iota, not a dot, will pass from the Law until all is accomplished" (Matthew 5:18). John refers to law in his letter to the Gentiles as, "For the law was given through Moses, grace and truth came to Jesus" (1:17).

The law that was passed to Moses is not obsolete for today nor does it mean salvation excludes one from it. Rather, "the giving of the law and the coming of Jesus Christ mark decisive events in the history of salvation. In the law, God graciously revealed His character and righteous requirements to the nation of Israel. Jesus, however marked the final definitive revelation of God" (ESV Study Bible 2020). In the book of John, a scenario is described whereby the rabbis and the religious of the Jewish society asked John the Baptist who he was. John writes,

> He confessed and did not deny, but confessed, 'I am not the Christ.' And they asked him, 'What then? Are you Elijah?' He said, 'I am not.' 'Are you the Prophet?' And he answered, 'No!' So they said to him, 'Who are you? We need an answer to those who sent us. What do you say to about yourself?' He said, 'I am the voice of one crying out in the wilderness. Make straight the way of the Lord' as the prophet Isaiah said' (1:20-23).

John the Baptist answers that he is just someone who is paving the way for the Messiah. Is this not what all Christians should be doing, paving the way for the second coming of the Lord? He will come to judge. Law serves to shed light on sin so that one can get on their knees and ask for forgiveness. Repentance leads to forgiveness by the grace of the Lord. Through the loving grace of God, we receive eternal life and are spared from His wrath on judgment day.

Donning the postmodern lens of reality interpretation and reading Galatians 5:18, which states, "if you are led by the Spirit, you are not under the law" may lead one to conclude that Mosaic Law no longer applies. An example of this is found in an up and coming pastor's opinion of the moral law. He opines, "A lot of preaching has been unwittingly, unconsciously seduced by moralism." According to his lens, "so many contemporary sermons strengthen this slavery to self" (Tchividjian 95).

On the "contrary, the New Testament heightens, not lessens the place of the moral law in the life of the believer for the indicative [that is, the doing of the gospel] has been heightened through Christ's mediatorical work" (Jones 38). As a consequence of antinomianism, sin, hell, and Satan are rarely touched upon in contemporary churches. Instead the carnality of Jesus is emphasized over His deity.

The Gospel is summarily watered down and where once certain behaviors of man were considered sin, they no longer are. An example is homosexuality. Prior to the 1960's, it was considered a sin. In roughly the ensuing next three decades, homosexuality was considered a mental disorder. Currently, homosexuality is normal demanding all the legal rights as heterosexuals. This example follows what Jesus warns in 1 Corinthians 5:6-7. It states, "Your boasting is not good. Do you not know that a little leaven leavens the whole lump? Cleanse out the old leaven that you may be a new lump, as you are really unleavened." Leaven used during Jesus' time and occasionally used today is fermented dough that is used to bake food products.

A piece of dough from the pre-baked product is kept to use for the next baking. In the case of homosexuality, what was once known as sin (the leaven) has leavened the dough (His word) infecting the faith. That little piece of leaven can deconstruct truth. In the book of Revelation, Jesus is described by John having "eyes like a flame of fire" and feet "like burnished bronze, refined in a furnace" (14, 15). "Christ is looking with pierced judgment on the Church because she has permitted false teaching to creep into her midst and 'mislead my servants'" (LaHaye 69).

Many within the theological elite do not consider deconstruction's action on meaning as being bad. The view is that a variety of interpretations many be edifying as it functions to bring believers together, encouraging each other in seeking truth (Poythress). What kind of truth is sought is disconcerting because in a postmodern society, truth is relative.

Deconstruction to the postmodern biblical exegete proves that a text can be interpreted in multiple ways, therefore there is no final meaning. According to them, the author of the text does not have the final say because their perspective is sourced within the language and culture of the day the text was written. Readers are also influenced by their context of language and cultures thereby, meaning is never constant (Poythress).

A case in point is in the highly respected contemporary New Testament scholar, N.T. Wright (1948). Wright has recently been making headway in the Reformed and Evangelical circles with his take on the Pauline epistles and the doctrine of justification. His book entitled *The New Perspective*, is increasingly being considered as the new hermeneutic of the New Testament. Wright's new standpoint of the New Testament centers on Paul's ministry in the area of righteousness of God, imputation and justification. Wright's argument is that up till now, theology in these areas has been largely been grounded in Western thinking.

Therefore, Western paradigm of thought must be excised in order to ascertain the milieu of Paul's teaching in order to arrive at the intended meaning in his teaching. I believe that to do so would present a linear reasoning into Paul's words and actions as opposed to a vertical one which seeks enlightenment by the Holy Spirit. To explain, an example in each of the three areas of Wright's focus is presented.

1) Righteousness of God – God is described as a Judge with the responsibility of seeing to it that law and order is maintained. According to Wright, "this 'righteousness' is of course in the form of justice; God has bound himself to the covenant, or perhaps...God's covenant is binding upon him, and through this covenant he has promised not only to save Israel, but

also, thereby to renew creation itself" (279). Indeed, God's righteousness is the "what" that distinguishes Him from any other god. But for Wright, that is as far as it goes. To consider beyond this point would infer imputation and divine justification. Both of which he explains away using forensic language. Wright maintains that Paul was speaking forensic language because of the environment during his time. The best way to clarify this is to use Wright's own words. He states,

> In the Jewish law court, Paul would have known, that there is no Director of Public Prosecutions; there is a judge with a plaintiff and a defendant appearing before him. When the case has been heard, the judge finds in favour of one party and against the other. Once that has happened, the vindicated party possesses the status 'righteous'- not itself a moral statement, we note, but a statement of how things stand in terms of the now- completed lawsuit...the judge's *own* righteousness has not been passed on to them, by imputation,

impartation, or any other process. What they have is a status of 'righteous' that comes *from* the judge. Let me stress, in particular, that when the judge finds in favour of one party or the other, he quite literally makes them righteous; because 'righteous' at this point is not the word denoting moral character, but only and precisely the status that you have when the court has found in your favour. If this had been kept in mind in earlier centuries a great deal of heartache and puzzle might have been avoided (280-281).

A stance like this negates what Paul writes to the church in Philippi. He states, "For his sake I have suffered the loss of all things and count them as rubbish, in order that I may gain Christ and be found in him, *not have a righteousness of my own that comes from the law,* but that which *comes through faith in Christ, the righteousness from God that depends on faith*" (8-9, my emphasis). This is confirmed in Romans 10:5-9 where it states, "For Moses writes about the righteousness that is based on the law, that the person who does the commandments shall live by them. But the righteousness based on faith says...'The word is near you, in your mouth and in your heart'...because if you confess with your mouth that Jesus is Lord and believe in your heart that God raised him from the dead, you will be saved." The horizontal logic does not explain God's righteousness in the death of His Son (Romans 3:21-26) nor the righteousness by faith (Romans 3:27-31).

2). Imputed Righteousness – Wright denies the interpretation of Philippians 3:9 and 2 Corinthians 5:21 which states, "For our sake he made him to be sin who knew no sin, so that in him we might become the righteousness of God." Wright's contention is that there is no imputed righteousness on those of faith. Only to those who are called "to be apostolic preachers actually embody God's own covenant faithfulness...This is not God's own righteousness, or Christ's righteousness, that is reckoned to God's people, but rather the fresh status of 'covenant member', and/or 'justified sinner,' and responded with the 'obedience of faith'" (281). Thus, righteousness, through the saving grace of God is not an identity one shares with the Lord but a membership in His covenant. Again, the thinking process displayed seems to center upon human as opposed to the Divine who is revealed via the Holy Spirit. Reading Scripture this way does not answer one glaring question. The question being, "If God can impute the sins of humanity on His Son for the sake of humanity, why can't He impute the righteousness wrought by His Son on those who believe?" Romans 5:9 states, "Since, therefore, we have now been justified by his blood, much more shall we be saved by him from the wrath of God." The imputation of righteousness saves from the wrath of God. If we don't have it, we die.

3). Justification- Wright wrote a book on justification entitled *Justification. God's Plan and Paul's Vision.* Again, Wright uses forensic language which he insists provides the framework to Paul's letters and in this case justification. A key passage on justification is found in Romans 5:16. It states, "The free gift is not like the result of that one man's sin. For the judgment following one trespass brought condemnation, but the free gift following many trespasses brought justification." The amazing grace of our Lord is apparent in paying the penalty of death brought on by the first earthly father. He condemned humanity by his disobedience for eternity. The Lord's intervention justified humanity once more to stand before Him. Although Wright acknowledges the love of God for humanity through the sacrifice of Jesus, it only shows the obedience of the Lord to His Father. Wright turns to Philippians 2:8 to confirm his position which states, "And being found in human form, he humbled himself by becoming obedient to the point of death."

In retort to Wright, does God's grace have any bearing on justification? Or to that fact, does it have any bearing on the salvation of mankind? Wright agrees that grace is the foundation of justification which God freely offers. Grace demonstrates the love of God. But I do not see the connection between divine grace and Paul's purported forensic language.

For the Wrights of the world who try to deconstruct the word of God, it flies in the face of what Paul said in the first letter to the Corinthians. The Corinthian church was plagued with divisiveness, sexual immorality and pride. The Gentile church as well as the Jewish ones would have had difficulty understanding Paul's words if they interpreted them using a worldly perspective. Paul explains it this way,

> And I, when I came to you, brothers, did not come proclaiming to you the testimony of God with lofty speech and wisdom. For I decided to know nothing among you except Jesus Christ and him crucified. And I was with you in weakness and in fear and much trembling and my speech and my message were not in plausible words of wisdom, but in demonstration of the Spirit and power, that your faith might not rest in the wisdom of men but in the power of God (2:1-5).

Paul makes it clear that he did not go to the Corinthians with a personal agenda but only to speak of what was revealed to him by the Holy Spirit. The words spoken by

Paul would only make sense to those who are filled by the Holy Spirit (1 Corinthians 1:18). Therefore,

> Among the mature we do impart wisdom, although it is not a wisdom of this age, who are doomed to pass away. But we impart a secret and hidden wisdom of God, which God decreed before the ages for our glory. None of the rulers of this age understand this, for if they had, they would not have crucified the Lord of glory. But, as it is written, 'What no eye has seen, nor ear heard, nor the heart of man imagined, what God has prepared for those who love him'- these things God has revealed to us through the Spirit. For the Spirit searches everything, even the depths of God (1 Corinthians 2:6-10).

If Paul would have indeed, spoken in a forensic language, those filled with the Holy Spirit would be scratching their heads. There is no horizontal logic here but a reasoning that comes vertically from the Lord. There is no need to deconstruct the Scripture for they are the words of God, the great Author of everything (2 Timothy 3:16-17).

Summary

The disputes presented illustrate the consequences of deconstruction upon thought and language in Christian theology. Deconstruction hopes to prove that there is no stable meaning but many, therefore, no truth. Acceptance of deconstruction will decimate Biblical truths in order to reconstruct them using philosophy that serves self.

Just like the serpent convinced Adam and Eve to disobey God, deconstruction is used to dupe mankind. The serpent asked one simple question, "Did God actually say...?" and mankind was plunged into darkness and death (Genesis 3). The "Wrights" of the world ask the same question regarding justification. They ask, "Did God really mean justification to refer how one becomes Christian? Could justification really mean how one knows a person is a Christian?" The subtle shift can send an innocent believer down the wrong path. The innocent believer who is not well acquainted with Scripture will fail to recognize that the focus is taken away from the change in heart one experiences via justification (1 Samuel 16:7). The focus relocates to the external, that is, works. The subtle shift becomes quite damaging. Under the influence of deconstruction, justification is eviscerated from any connection to spirituality, the resultant being works, credos and legalism.

"Jesus is the same yesterday and today and forever. Do not be led away by diverse and strange teachings, for it is good for the heart to be strengthened by grace, not by foods, which have not benefited those devoted to them" (Hebrew 13:8-9). Do not depart from the truth in God's words. It is better to feast on the grace and truth of God than to any lofty teaching, doctrine or tradition served by man. The passage attests to Jesus's steadfastness and His grace sustains. Whereas, anything other than what He offers, is a lost cause.

V.   JESUS IS TRUTH...NOT! A STUDY

A study was done using scientific methodology to lend credence to the thesis presented thus far. The thesis is a language exists within a language. The contention is that the meaning within language has been changed. Language has been placed into the scientific realm whereby man can potentially manipulate it for its own use.

Over the years, words have taken up new meaning but of late, there has been a hurried pace with increased efforts. This is evident in the wide disparity between the present and later generations. Therefore, as far as Christianity is concerned, the urgency is to learn the language within language in order to minister to the lost.

As it was in the beginning with the building of the tower of Babel (Genesis 11:1-9), the project continues today.

Recent efforts to study language in humans, its acquisition, use and meanings have accelerated as science has increased its capability to understand nature. In the past, language was understood as part of a particular society and through language its culture could be ascertained. But a cognitive concept revolution developed in the 1950's and assisted by science reshaped linguistic theories. A new paradigm of thinking about language evolved with the perspective that language is to be considered as infinite manifestations of expressions with its own unique sounds and meanings. Expressions develop with their special characteristics within a system of thought and communication.

Linguistic study is directed to the inner workings of the mind and how it interprets meanings of expressions and sounds, their communication and the various uses of language. The experience of speaking a language is the expression of the language. Viewed in this light, language is dislocated from man and puts it into a category by itself. Hence, language is considered an organ. No surprise here since it was Charles Darwin (1809-1882), the author of the theory of human evolution, who considered language as an intricate and mutually dependent organism. The claim is that languages as dependent organisms go through the same process of selection (recall the theory of natural selection) as man progresses.

Language perceived as an organism gives scientists the license to experiment and manipulate it. The scientists operate under the assumption that like any organism, there are specific characteristics that are shared by each genre of organisms. In the case of language, it is argued that language shares a collective grammar that is standard across all languages.

On the contrary, in foundational Christian theology, God is considered the originator/author of language with meanings based and measured according to His words. So powerful are God's words that He only spoke and the world as well as man was created (Genesis

1:6, 8-11, 14-26). When Moses doubted his ability to petition Pharaoh for the release of the Israeli nation, God said, "Who made man's mouth? Who made him mute, or deaf, or seeing or blind?" (Exodus 4:11) Throughout Scripture, language was integral in revealing God.

The scientific methodology used in this study is called Grounded Theory Methodology. The purpose of the grounded theory method is to build theory that is conducive to and highlights the phenomenon under study. The process of grounded theory is one that lends itself to the illumination and examination of areas of concern. This is achieved through the use of data that ordinarily are not quantifiable, for example, interviews, observations and written documents.

Grounded theory as a methodology was originally developed by two sociologists: Barney Glaser and Anselm Strauss. Analyzing data by the grounded theory method entails reducing raw data into concepts which are designed to stand for categories. The categories are then developed and integrated into theory. The process is broken down into steps, each one building upon the other. Generated data are analyzed, ordered, recorded and stored in a manner that is retrievable and usable. Techniques to retrieve information at a moment's notice include coding, memoing and diagraming. "In coding, the incidents and facts are marked in some way, either underscoring or circling, and are rewritten in an abstracted process.

They show the theory developing step by step. They allow the analyst to keep a record and to order the results of the analysis. They also enable the analyst to know where he or she has been, is now and needs to go in the future of the research" (Corbin 103, 108). In memoing, the researcher writes accounts of observations and responses during data analysis and theory development. Diagrams are visual representations of the researcher's analytical scheme. Techniques to retrieve information involve three types of coding;

1. Open coding – data generated via line-by-line analysis is broken down, examined, compared

and conceptualized according to properties and dimensional locations.

2. Axial coding – specificity is supplied to the categories in terms of the conditions that give rise to them, the specific set of properties and the action/interactional strategies. Axial coding also considers how the data is handled, managed, carried out and the outcomes or results of the actions and interactions.

3. Selective-coding – the process of selecting the core category, systemically relating it to other categories, validating those relationships and filling gaps in categories that need further refinement and development.

Literature review as a technique in grounded theory research is approached as a source of data as well as a means to raise questions about the validity and reliability of the data. The literature is compared to the analytic concepts and relationships in the developing theory. In this study, the Bible is considered as a reference and part of the literature review (Osso, *Knowing*).

The Method of Inquiry: Applied

The grounded theory approach in data analysis seeks to identify meanings attributed to words to pinpoint a thinking process(s). Data is collected systematically and analyzed, word for word, using the method set forth.

Sample and Setting

In the study, the perspectives of young teenagers was sought. The sample size consisted of twelve consenting teens born between the years 1997-2002. Six were males, six were females. The sample is regarded as the Millennial generation or Gen Y. According to the Barna Research Group, due to the varied viewpoints, relationship, modes of learning and others that characterize this age group, they are labeled as Mosaics. Data gathering was in individuals' homes. The researcher was not present during data gathering deferring the administration of the test to the proxy.

Informed Consent and Ethical Issues

To obtain formal consent to conduct the study, the researcher via the proxy verbally asked parents as well as the teen's permission to participate in the research. The purpose of the study as well as the research procedures were explained. A verbal consent and participation in the study sufficed as a formal consent. The accord addressed the following areas:

- Where and how the researcher will utilize the setting.

- How often and for how long the research will continue.

- When will the researcher leave the setting.

- How the researcher will share the information.

- How the researcher will assure accurate portrayal.

- What will the researcher do if the direction of the research changes.

- What the researcher will do with unanticipated findings.

- What will the researcher do with secrets and confidential material.

- What will the researcher do with inclusion and exclusion of information (Osso, *Knowing*). Individuals in the study were made aware that they were free to withdraw at any time.

Data Collection

Data collection utilized a Word Association Test that was constructed by the researcher (See Appendix). The research tool was based on Word Association Tests that Dr. Carl Jung (1875-1961) devised. Jung was a renowned psychologist famous for being one of the founders of analytic psychology. His Word Association Tests were developed as a tool to delve into the subconscious mind of man. In Jung's tests, a set of words somewhat related was administered to a patient. The patient responded to a word, one at a time, with the first word that came to mind. The time between reading the word and responding was timed. Based on the associated word and the time interval, a personality trait was determined.

In this study, the Word Association Test consisted of two sets of words that are loosely related. The participants were asked to respond to each word with the first word that came to mind. But instead of timing the response interval as in Jung's test, the participants were asked to rate the word.

The purpose of this rating was to measure the worth or value of the word to the participant, that is, how strong does the meaning of the word hold for the participant. The rating scale for all words in the test is; 1 – strongly feel, 2 – moderately feel, 3 – little or no feeling. All words in the sets and phrases used in the test wer based on research during the review of literature. The words, phrases and specific directions selected for the Word Association Test is an attempt to get a wholistic perspective of the sample group.

A third set of words were presented in pairs. The participant was asked to circle the one word that appealed to him/her. A couple of Bible verses were also presented. The verses were not identified as Scriptural ones. The participant was asked to write the first word that came to mind upon reading the verse. Lastly, the participant was asked to write down four words that described him/herself.

Data Analysis

Throughout data analysis, the method of coding was employed. The coding involves the operation of breaking down, conceptualizing and organizing data into a theory. Analysis in grounded theory is composed of three types of coding: open, axial and selective. In open coding, each word was analyzed. The coding was guided by certain questions such as, "What is the commonality in the responses, that is, is there a common meaning? How is it rated? Is there a gender difference in the responses? An example of open coding and how it was documented is presented. The word is REST.

The responses to REST were tired, sleep, pool and bed.

8/12 sleep. All gave it a 1 rating (Male-16, M-16, M-15, M-16, Female-15, F-15, F-14, F-16).

1/12 sleep Number 3 rating (M-17).

1/12 pool. Number 1 rating (M-17).

1/12 bed. Number 2 rating (M-16).

1/12 tired. Number 3 rating (F-15).

After open coding, specificity in processes was pursued by going over the data repeatedly looking for relationships in terms of properties, action/interaction strategies and consequences of actions and interactions. An example of axial coding and its documentation is the word FREEDOM.

5/12 strongly felt freedom as a sign or symbol such as flag, American, flag. Whereas, two participants responded with open and fun. These could describe a state of being. 7/12 had moderately, little or no feeling. Again, freedom signified as sign or symbol and state of being.

The majority of participants do not regard freedom as something integral. Jesus became man so that He could pay the price for sin which keeps one in bondage, a slave. Through Jesus, one is then liberated from sin, bondage, slavery and darkness. One is free!

Selective coding takes place when the core process is identified by systematically relating the other processes. This is accomplished when the core process can explicate a narrative that can be validated against data. The narrative can fill in processes that may need further refinement and/or development. In this study, the core process identified helped to explain how and why participants chose the answers on the word association test. The core process that emerged from the word association test is the following:

Who I am is defined by an experience of spirituality as well as knowledge by belonging to a community, a social event that allows for relationships and being true to oneself, both of

which explain the how and what. My identity is tied to family as well as friends. I seek a big brother and respect the liberal and law alike.

Figure 1 is a diagram that assisted in the identification of the core process.

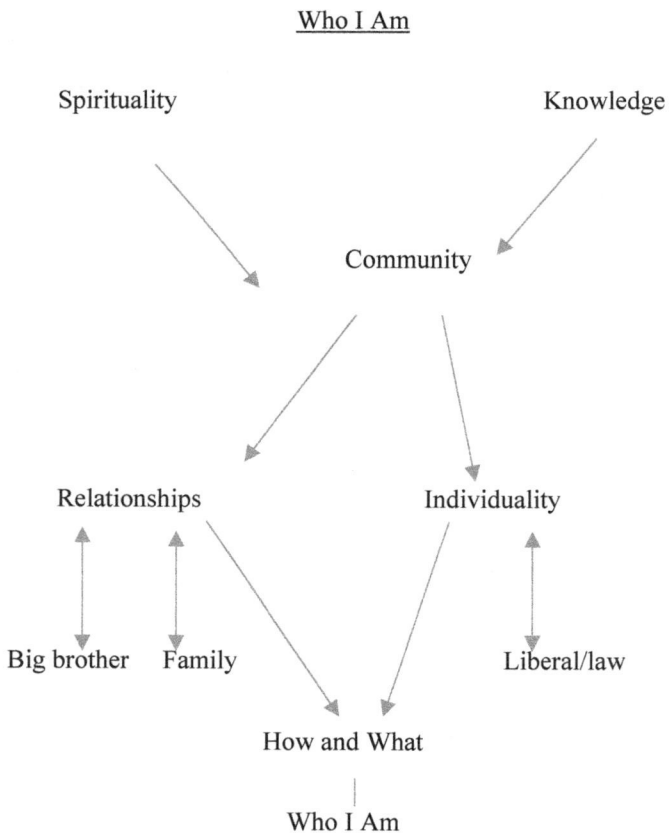

Who I Am

Spirituality   Knowledge

Community

Relationships   Individuality

Big brother   Family   Liberal/law

How and What

Who I Am

Figure 1

Credibility of the Study

Credibility measures how vivid and faithful the description of the process is in relation to the phenomenon being studied. The rigor of grounded theory methodology, through its coding procedures, ensures careful recording and data generation. Analysis of the data and the development of the processes were guided by the researcher's past experience employing grounded theory methodology. Foremost was awareness of the risk of subjectivity as the data was analyzed. The concern was aptly identified so that its effect on the study could be noted and controlled appropriately. To insure auditability, all data and analytic decisions are available.

Research Findings

The research findings found that the alternative name, Mosaic, given to the Millennial generation is quite apropos. Mosaics bring diverse opinions, feelings and thoughts to a certain entity as would a medley of small tiles come together to form a whole picture. According to Kinnaman, Mosaics are extraordinarily relational as well as narcissistic. Relationships encompass both positive and negative ones. The current research results proved to be so. A polemic was found in the core process that reflected a hegemony between self (me) and community (others). The data generated by the Word Association Test served to arrive at the core process. The individual parts of the test can be viewed as subprocesses of the core process. There were no gender differences in the responses.

Beginning with the first of the two sets of individual words, the words were loosely linked with a meaning that may be linked to being, that is, the makeup of a person. As part of being, four fruits of the Holy Spirit were included in the word association test. They were love, peace, compassion and joy. The resultant data collected is the following.

Love, peace and joy were strongly felt (rated as 1) by 7/12 of the research participants. Love was widely held by 11/12 of the participants. Whereas 5/12 of the participants felt strongly with compassion. Compassion clearly held a moderate attachment with one rating it with little or no feeling.

Love: Love was rated highly. Love was noted in relationships with the opposite sex and family. Such relationships were described as heart, happy and warmth. *The outstanding words associated with love, in descending order were sex, heart and Mom.*

Peace: Peace received varied responses with two participants associating it with love, two with dove and two with hippie. The rest of the participants noted happiness, sign, beat generation, world, utopia and tea. *The words closely associated with peace were love, dove and hippie.*

Joy: Half of the participants associated joy with happy. Two responded with love. The rest noted Christmas, smile and swimming. *Happy and love were the top words associated with joy.*

Compassion: Half of participants responded to the word compassion with love. Five of the twelve rated the response with one. Outstanding among the results was that

7/12 rated compassion with moderate and little or no feeling. Compassion was not a priority although 11/12 associated it with *love* and one associated it with care.

The words, soul, spirit and heart were also part of the first word association group. The intent here by the researcher was to gain a deeper understanding of self. **Soul** was rated one, strongly felt, by 7/12 of the participants but each had a different associated word. Their words were amazing, life, spirit, food, dance, person and God. Three out of the 12 participants rated soul with two, a moderate feeling. The words noted for soul were life, human and ghosts. The rest, 2/12 rated soul with one. They responded with cycle and search. Of all the varied associated words, *the outstanding word out was life.*

The word **spirit** was met with divided responses with half noting (1) a strong feeling with the word and two associating it with God. The rest of the associated words were ghost, soul, and dance. Three of the twelve participants gave spirit a moderate rating and associated it with holy, animal and free. Two participants rated spirit

(3), little or no feeling. In this group, one associated it with ghost while the other gave no response. *Among the words associated with spirit, God was the common response and one with no response.*

Heart was met with 5/12 strongly favoring it with two participants associating it with soul. The rest of the words noted for heart were sweet, love and valentine. Six of the 12 participants rated heart with moderate feeling and six different associated words. They were soul, love, red, happy, body and ache. One participant rated heart with little or no feeling and organ as their associated word. *In the end, soul was the most associated word for heart.*

The rest of the first set of words consisted of random words that can be found in the Bible in numerous contexts. They were freedom, hate, forgive, revenge, grateful, angry, guilty and rest. The words were grouped into two categories. The first category consisted of freedom, rest, grateful and forgive. The other was guilty, hate, revenge and angry. The following are the results.

Freedom: Five of the twelve participants highly rated freedom. Four of the twelve gave it a moderate rating. Two had little or no feeling. *The top associated words for freedom were American and flag with two rating it with little or no feeling.*

Grateful: Half of the participants rated the word grateful with strongly felt. Four of the twelve rated it moderately while one had little or no feeling. Another did not rate their response. Five of the twelve participants associated grateful with thankful. Two noted it with parents. The rest associated grateful with appreciative, genuine, Mom, family and humans. *The outstanding associated words were thankful (with one receiving no rating) and parents.*

Forgive: A plethora of associated words characterized the response to the word forgive. Half were rated with (1), strongly felt to words such as forget, love, friendly, friends and me. Three of the participants rated the word forgive, with little or no feeling. They responded with the words forget, friend and makeup. Two marked their responses with a moderate feeling and associated it with the words, forget and peace. One participant did not respond. *Forget and friends were the two words that predominated and one participant that did not respond.*

Rest: Nine of the twelve participants had strong feelings with the word rest. Eight of them associated it with *sleep.* The rest of the responses were pool, bed and tired.

The first set of words also contained the words guilty, hate, revenge and angry. The data generated in this subset of words are the following;

Guilty: Seven of the twelve participants gave a strong rating for the word guilty. Two associated it with conscience, the rest with afraid, upset, lying, court and prison. Three of the participants had a moderate feeling towards the word guilty and they responded with the words lying, sorrow and murder. Two had little or no feeling. They associated it with jewelry and court. *The prominent associated words for guilty were conscience, lying and court.*

Hate: The rating for this word was divisive. Half of the participants strongly felt the word and associated it with fight, school, Robby (a proper noun) and anger. Two responded with like and love. Four of the participants gave the word hate, a little or no feeling rating. Their associated words were lie, anger, let go and pain. One rated hate as moderately felt and connected it with envy, another did not respond at all. *Anger was the top associated word with hate.*

Revenge: Five participants rated the word revenge with a strong feeling. Associated words comprised of two noting anger. The others replied with enemy, justice and movies. Five felt little or no feeling towards revenge and associated it with stupid, backfire, pretty little liars (assuming it is referring to a T.V. program) and scheme. Two had a moderate feeling towards the word. Their words for revenge were hatred and guilt. *Therefore, the outstanding associated word for revenge is anger.*

Angry: Strong feelings for the word angry were noted in 5/12 of the participants. Two associated the word with mad, two with red and one participant noted upset.

Four participants rated angry with little or no feeling. In this group, angry was connected with mad, hate (by two participants) and lastly birds (assuming this means the on-line game application). Three of the participants rated the word angry with a moderate feeling. Words noted with it were aggressive, unhappy and men. *The top associated words for angry were mad, red and hate.*

The second set of words in the word association test are those that may be antithetical to a postmodern society. According to Kinnaman's study, Mosaics are skeptical of authority and societal institutions. He describes them as having "nothing negative to say about their parents or the Bible but they [see] little connection between these sources of authority and their attitudes or behavior. This finding suggest that many young people maintain split selves – they are capable of holding contradictory beliefs and behavior in multiple, even conflicting categories" (52). The following research words were presented to the participants in no specific order except for the word, truth. It was noted in two place in the set of words. This was done deliberately.

Truth orders the way one lives, everything hinges on truth. Due to truth's precarious standing in postmodern society, the placement of truth twice in the word association test served as confirmation in the participants' response.

Church: Seven of the twelve participants felt strongly with the word church. Four of the seven participants associated it with God while the rest noted it with communion, faith and Sunday. Three of the twelve participants rated church as moderately felt associating it with religion, boring and Christ. Two had little or no feeling, citing religion and steeple. *The dominant words for church were God and religion.*

Law: The ratings were dramatic for the word law. Six of the twelve participants held a strong feeling, four of the twelve had little or no feeling and two had moderate feeling. Of the six participants with strong feeling, their words associated with law were rules by two and the rest were police, court, order and attorney. The four who noted little or no feeling associated law with rules, attorney, judge and the statement, "I am the law." The last two with a moderate feeling rating responded with rules and school. *Rules and attorney were the top words associated with law.*

Friend: Five of the twelve participants rated the word friend as highly felt. Five rated it with moderate feeling and two had little or no feeling. The participants that had a strong feeling with the word friend, replied with five different associated words. They were trust, friendship, love, hangouts and "the nine" (assuming it is the name of a group).

The other five participants also had five different responses. They were love, party, companion, loyal and care. The remaining two connected friend with family and enemy. Further clarification of the associated word enemy, was sought. Turning to the phrase, "Love your enemies," the response was compared to the word given for that phrase. The associated word was forgive. This might be an example of holding onto two dichotomies as noted in Kinnaman's research (friend > enemy < forgive). *Although there was a diversity of words associated with friend, the one word that barely stood above the others was love.*

Family: Eight participants rated a strong feeling with the word family, three noting love. The rest associated family with blood, welcomed, loving, cousins and "the nine." Three participants had a moderate feeling with the word family. Their words for family were friends, party and first. One participant noted little or no feeling with the word and associated family with friends. *The dominant words for family were love/loving and friends.*

Knowledge: Knowledge was highly rated by six participants. Three associated it with school and the rest with smart, power and me. Four noted a moderate feeling for knowledge with two connecting it with smart. The rest responded with school and power. Two gave knowledge a little or no feeling rating. School and power were its associated words. *The primary associated words for knowledge were school, smart and power.*

Religion: Five participants rated the word religion with strongly felt. Two of the five associated it with God, the rest with Christian, class and elements. Four of the twelve gave the word religion a moderately felt rating and associated it with God, church, good and optional. Three noted a little or no feeling towards the word religion. Two noted religion. One responded with Pope. *The predominant associated word for religion was God and church.*

Truth: Four out of the twelve participants rated the word truth as strongly felt. All responded with the same word in both places where the word truth was cited. Their responses to the word truth in both areas were: fun/happy, lie/lie, rightful/rightful, honesty/honesty. There was a split or contradictory rating noted in two of the participants. They rated the word truth one time with strongly felt and another with moderate feeling. Four participants rated the word truth as moderately felt with one split rating. They noted moderate feeling the first time and little or no feeling the second time. The associated words for truth in this group were false/false, conclusion/valid. The split rating were for freedom/freedom. There were no low ratings. But two participants skipped the word truth in both places. *The primary words associated with truth were lie, false, honesty* *(with two participants opting out). Note that the two top associated words for truth were lie and false, its antithesis.*

Justice: Participants were divided with 8/12 rating the word justice as strongly felt and 4/12 with little or no feeling. Three of the eight participants associated the word justice with law while two responded with peace. The rest choose league, world and truth. The other participants with a low rating associated the word justice with happy, truth, court and freedom. *The dominant words connected with the word justice were law, power and truth. (Note that justice was not an associated word for truth).*

Power: Associated words with power were varied except for two who noted strength. Seven participants felt strongly about the word power and used God, leader, forward, attention, respect, friends and king to associate with the word. Four participants rated the word justice as moderately felt. Two participants in this group noted strength, the rest were rule and me. One participant rated justice with little or no feeling and connected it with yield.

The outstanding word associated with the word power is strength.

Enemy: The rating for enemy consisted of 4/12 as strongly felt, 5/12 as moderately felt and 3/12 with little or no feeling. For the high rating group, the associated words for enemy were hate by two participants, one responded with friend and the other replied with the word against. The group that rated the word enemy with a moderate feeling responded with words such as hate, foe, friend, villain and evil. The last group with a low rating associated the word enemy with friend, frenemy and kill. To further clarify the standing of these associated words in the group that gave the words a number 3 rating, they were cross referenced with the phrase in the test, "Love your enemies." The individual words used to respond to the phrase by the three participants were Jesus, "friend" and hate. Jesus corresponded to friend, "friend" corresponded with frenemy and hate with kill. Therefore, assumption is made that the meanings of the associated words are constant. *The dominant associated word for enemy were friend,* *frenemy and hate. Interestingly, the primary associated word for enemy is its antithesis, friend.*

Sacrifice: Four participants rated the word sacrifice with little or no feeling. Their associated words were food, lamb, war and ultimate. Three of the twelve participants rated the word sacrifice with moderately felt. Two in this group identified love and one cited death. The three remaining participants highly rated the word sacrifice. Two noted love and the other give. *Love was the primary word associated with sacrifice but outstanding was the low rating.*

Judge: Five of the twelve participants highly rated the word judge. Three participants associated the word with court. The other two were wrong and Judy (assuming Judge Judy, a television program). Four participants rated the word judge, with number two, moderate. Judy and court were noted as well as exclude and ostracize. Three rated the word judge with little or no feeling. This group responded with court, not and law. *Court and Judy were the predominate words associated with judge.*

Reject: Rating for the word reject, was evenly divided among the participants but there were twelve different associated words. The group that highly rated reject cited disapprove, college, refuse and "reject" ed. The middle group noted the words dad, bye, outcast and foil. (The words strikes a chord of emotion such as sadness). The last group with the lowest rating responded with hate, lies, mean and clique. (The words elicit an emotion of bitterness). *There were no outstanding associated word for the word reject except for three evenly divided opinions about its worth. The last two ratings for reject demonstrated an emotional connection.*

The next part of the Word Association Test consisted of circling the word that was most appealing. The words used were based on the literature review. Some of the words were repeated in order to gain a better understanding of a process, if any. Analysis of the responds aided in the development of a core process. The responses consisted of the following:

- Spirituality (7/12) vs. Religion (5/12)

- Faith (3/12) vs. Experience (9/12)

- Knowledge (11/12) vs. Wisdom (1/12)

- Individual (5/12) vs. Community (7/12)

- Beliefs (5/12) vs. Belonging (7/12)

- Belonging (0) vs. Identity(12/12)

- Liberal (6/12) vs. Law (6/12)

- Where am I (1/12) vs. Who am I (11/12)

- Personal (4/12) vs. Social (8/12)

- How (6/12) vs. What (6/12)

- Relationship (6/12) vs. Being true to oneself (6/12)

- Family (10/12) vs. Friends (2/12)

- Teacher (3/12) vs. Friend (9/12)

- Big brother (8/12) vs. Friends (4/12)

Another component of the Word Association Test involved noting the first word that came to mind after reading two sentences. The two sentences were two Bible verses. The verses proved to serve a dual purpose, referred to in order to clarify a meaning in a seemingly contradictory word association situation. The other purpose was to ascertain any Christian influence **"Love**

your enemies" (Matthew 5:44) was associated with twelve different words. They were God, Jesus, hate, war, Bible, smart, equality, "friends," wrong, "friends," forgive and NO (No was intentionally capitalized). *Of the twelve words, five were contrary to the verse. The words were hate, war, wrong, "friends" and NO.*

The second sentence (verse) was **"Judge not and you will not be judged"** (Matthew 7:1*). Two participants associated the verse with God. The rest of the words were confusing, hypocrites, truth, friends, valid, fair, counselor, judge, college and rules.* Lastly the test asked the participants to write down four words that described themselves. The purpose of this exercise was to better understand the person who took the time out to contribute to this study. Words used on more than one occasion were; outgoing, generous, creative, caring, loving, fun, happy, nice, smart, social, intelligent, and loyal. Other words used were different, short, joyful, just, human, friendly, man, power, knowledge, athletic, honest, tall, sensitive, wild, beautiful, big, and handsome. *Based on the responses, the* *conclusion can be made that the participants had a positive attitude about themselves.*

Summary

The purpose of the research is to develop a theory that would lend credence to the premise that a language exists within language. A recent Barna study sheds light upon the present Mosaic generation's lack of understanding when it involves the words of God. The contention is that language that is presently spoken to explain/spread the Good News is not understood by the Mosaic generation. The meanings of the words have changed. Therefore, when the Good News is shared, the Mosaics' response is, "You lost me."

In the research a sample size of twelve participants reflective of the Mosaic generation contributed by engaging in a Word Association Test. The test was constructed by the researcher based on literature review. Data analysis was done by employing grounded theory methodology. Through this methodology, data analysis identified a core process that may explain why Mosaics have difficulty understanding the Good News. This finding is huge because as Kinnaman writes,

> The spiritual lives of millions of young people are at stake. That fact, in and of itself, should be reason enough to care. A person sets his or her moral and spiritual foundation early in life, usually before the age of thirteen, yet the teen and young adult years are significant period of experimentation, of testing the limits and reality of those foundations. In other words, even though the childhood and early adolescent years are the time during which spiritual and moral compasses are calibrated, the experimental and experiential decade from high school to the late twenties is the time when a young person's spiritual trajectory is confirmed and clarified (31)

Analysis of the data revealed a core process which states,

Who I am is defined by an experience of spirituality as well as knowledge by belonging to a community, a social event that allows relationships and being true to oneself, both of which explain the how and what. My identity is tied to family as well as friends. I seek a big brother and respect the liberal and law alike.

Further review of the data revealed a common word, that is, love. Love can be designated as the foundation that directs the core process. Under love, there were other words ranked lower than it. They were sex, joy, friend, family. God, sacrifice and compassion came next at a lower level. All the words were connected to love as subprocesses of love (Figure 2). Another schemata (Figure 3) demonstrates these subprocesses as they contribute to the core process.

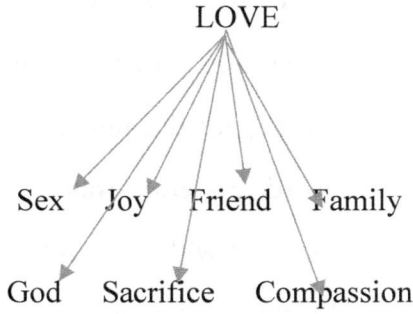

Figure 2.

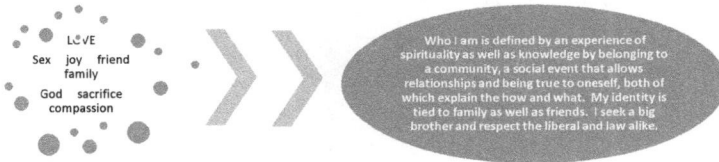

Figure 3.

Conspicuous in the research was the refusal by two participants to engage with the word truth. Two participants chose to negate any contribution with the word sacrifice. Another participant did not recognize the word forgive. The test word grateful, was not rated by a participant but associated it with thankful. The omissions are to be considered just important as the data, if not more significant. Is the blank space next to the test word due to the participant incomprehension of the word or is it because there is an unresolved internal conflict that prevents a response? The next chapter will discuss the data and the analysis along with recommendations.

VI.   DISCUSSION

From a scientific perspective, the research can be explained by looking at MRI results with cognitive variances occurring during Word Association Tests.   The MRI studies presented in the previous chapter stated that "Analysis showed how conflict takes place between the left and the right brain over three seconds, after which the left brain takes over to ensure 'hot buttons' will continue to be active" (Wiley 10/4/14).

Upon reading or hearing a word, that is the hot button, a battle takes place between the left and the right sides of the brain.   The left side of the brain triumphs over the right side of the brain in order to continue the drama that the hot button created.   This is interesting since the word for left in Latin is sinistra and is the root for the English word, sinister. Throughout history the left of anything was considered wrong. For example, writing with the left hand was considered improper as well as eating with the left hand. In the Bible, the Lord will separate the sheep from the goats at the last judgment. The sheep will go to His right and the goats will go to His left (Matthew 25:33). Also, Jesus sits at the right hand of God, not at the left.

The root word for right comes from old English. The word refers to what is good, moral, upstanding and proper (Etymology Dictionary, accessed 1/13/15). Much is said about the word right in Scripture, beginning with the Lord whose "righteousness and justice are the foundation of [His] throne" (Psalm 89:14).

As far as man is concerned, at one time, he was condemned "because of man's [Adam's] trespass, death reigned through that one man, much more will those who receive the abundance of grace and the free gift of righteous reign in life through one man Jesus Christ" (Romans 5:17).

The dichotomy that exists between the left and the right is indeed a matter of life and death.

Apply this observation to the activity of the brain documented on MRI, a supposition can be made that the left side of the brain represents the flesh, self or spiritually as the outer man who is not in accord with God. The left side of the brain can represent lawlessness and rebellion against God. According to Scripture, "the mystery of lawlessness is already at work" (2 Thessalonians 2:7). It can be also inferred that indeed, we have the genetic make-up by the DNA of our first parents Adam and Eve.

Man has the genetic disposition to defy God which keeps man in endless conflict with God. The flesh or the outer man (left side of the brain) rules man's life until man is reborn and takes on the Spirit of God. "Do you not know if you present yourselves to anyone as obedient slaves, you are slaves of the one whom you obey, either of sin, which leads to death, or of obedience, which leads to righteousness?" (Romans 6:16-17). The left side of the brain could very well represent the flesh or the genetic trait that is inherited from man's original earthly parents that Scripture speaks about. The ruling of the flesh brings one to sin and sin leads one to death. "For while we are living in the flesh, our sinful passions, aroused by the law were at work in our members to bear fruit for death" (Matthew 7:5).

Paul explains in the book of Romans, "But thanks be to God, that you who were once slaves to sin have become obedient from the heart to the standard of teaching to which you were committed, and having been set free from sin, have become slaves of righteousness" (6:17-18). The transformation of the heart takes place when one is reborn, saved or regenerated.

The right hemisphere of the brain may be the part of man that represents that which is made in the image of God (Genesis 1:26). After the fall of man by way of Adam, evil entered the world and man's temptation by Satan continued (Genesis 6:5). The left side of the brain dominates and battles with the right side. Peter expresses it this way. "Beloved, I urge you as sojourners and exiles to abstain from the passions of the flesh, which wage war against your soul" (1 Peter 2:11). If Christians are aware of this internal struggle and strive to crucify the flesh, how much more is the struggle for the unbeliever or the uniformed Christian? The struggle is reflective in society and even in the Christian churches.

Evidence of this is found in the detour from heeding the Word of God found in Scripture to a translation of it that is mindful of the prevailing culture in society. There is a whole scale rejection of propositional truth in favor of a redefinition of truth that is relative. The following graph helps to visualize the perspective.

Truth

Propositional truth	Redefined truth
Originates in God	Truth is what you make
Transcendent	Socially determined
Absolute	Consensual
Certainty	Relevant
Objective	Subjective
Authoritative	Communal or social

Figure 4.

Compare the current worldly definition of truth with what the book of John records in the life of Jesus. Since Jesus is both man and God, He is perfect. Therefore, the words He spoke as He dwelt among us are true. He states in His high priestly prayer to His Father, "For I have given them the words that you gave me, and they have received them and have come to know the truth that I came from you, and they have believed that you sent me" (17:8).

Later Jesus asks God to "Sanctify them in truth, your word

is truth" (17:17). Having the truth of God's word,

Christians will live their lives, have the mindset and speak

according to His word.

The Greek word for truth in 17:8 is *alethos* which

means certainly. The word is used as an adverb (Mounce).

In this context, the word truth is employed to qualify or

substantiate the words that Jesus spoke. In 17:17 the Greek

word for truth is *aletheia* which is the noun word for truth

(Mounce). Here, truth stands alone without measure or

standard to which it needs to qualify, validate or conform

to. Truth is with a capital T. Therefore to know Jesus (and

His words) is to know Truth. Jesus and truth are

synonymous for He is "the way, and the truth, and the life"

(John 14:6).

The blank space left by some participant next to the

word truth in the Word Association Test is a serious

concern. The implication of this raises many questions.

Could the Word Association Test results indicate the

struggle between the left and right hemispheres of the brain, between good and evil? Does ignorance of truth exist? Does the silence represent the transformation of propositional truth to mean something else? Could the silence regarding truth indicate the battle that arises within as "hot buttons" words such as sacrifice and forgive are heard or read?

The Bible instructs mankind about the struggle between good and evil but can Word Association Tests scientifically provide insight into the struggle? For example, love is the greatest fruit seen in a person as a result of the indwelling Holy Spirit (Galatians 5:22, 1 Corinthians 13:13) and faith works through love (Galatians 5:6). If there is no faith, then what kind of love is at work? The research study showed that love works through a spirit of lust which seeks self–gratification. The vertical pattern of love that seeks God the Father is turned to community, parents and friends. It seems that the left brain succeeds in maintaining the tension as well as the power over the right side of the brain.

Could universal grammar, which according to Chomsky is inherent in the genetic make-up of man, be the driving force in part, for the activity of the left hemisphere of the brain? Truth has certainly been deconstructed to a level where it can be taught as a grammar. The language faculty center of the brain receives this grammar and a reality is established that is perceived as truth.

The person reveals the "truth" by the way the person lives and thinks. Christians are guilty of assuming the grammar that is not of God as evidenced by their acceptance of homosexuality, abortion, Insider Movement and other liberal agendas. The tragedy in this type of grammar is that well -meaning Christians think they are doing good deeds. God's grammar can also be taught. The grammar is contained within the pages of Scripture. The language within language of the other needs to be learned in order to teach God's grammar.

Sacrifice

The word sacrifice was also overlooked by two of the participants. The same questions that arose with the omission of truth are applicable here. The difference here is that these participants were not the same ones who bypassed the word truth. Sacrifice is a word that can characterize the New Testament and it basically means putting forth for the other at a cost. Whether one believes the story of Jesus or not, all will have to concede that Jesus exemplified the true model of sacrifice. He humbled Himself to become man so that "he himself likewise partook of the same things that through death he might destroy the one who has the power of death, that is, the devil and deliver all those who through fear of death were subject to lifelong slavery" (Hebrews 2:14-15).

John Piper, a popular contemporary Baptist pastor and author wrote a small book entitled *Fifty Reasons Why Jesus Came to Die*. Each short chapter explains a reason.

Together, the chapters encapsulate the meaning of sacrifice in Jesus Christ. They are:

1. To Absorb the Wrath of God

2. To Please His Heavenly Father

3. To Learn Obedience and Be Perfected

4. To Achieve His Own Resurrection from the Dead

5. To Show the Wealth of God's Love and Grace for Sinners

6. To Show His Own Love for Us

7. To Cancel the Legal Demands of the Law Against Us

8. To Become Ransom for Many

9. For the Forgiveness of Our Sins

10. To Provide the Basis for Our Justification

11. To Complete the Obedience That Becomes Our Righteousness

12. To Take Away Our Condemnation

13. To Abolish Circumcision and All Rituals as the Basis of Salvation

14. To Bring Us to Faith and Keep Us Faithful

15. To Make Us Holy, Blameless, and Perfect

16. To Give Us a Clear Conscience

17. To Obtain for Us All Things That are Good for Us

18. To Heal Us from Moral and Physical Sickness

19. To Give Eternal Life to All Who Believe on Him

20. To Deliver Us from the Present Evil Age

21. To Reconcile Us to God

22. To Bring Us to God

23. So That We Might Belong to Him

24. To Give Us Confident Access to the Holiest Place

25. To Become for Us the Place Where We Meet God

26. To Bring the Old Testament Priesthood to an End and Become the Eternal High Priest

27. To Become a Sympathetic and Helpful Priest

28. To Free Us from the Futility of Our Ancestry

29. To Free Us from the Slavery of Sin

30. That We Might Die to Sin and Live to Righteousness

31. So That We Would Die to the Law and Bear Fruit for God

32. To Enable Us to Live for Christ and Not Ourselves

33. To Make the Cross the Ground of All Our Boasting

34. To Enable Us to Live by Faith in Him

35. To Give Marriage Its Deepest Meaning

36. To Create a People Passionate for Good Works

37. To Call Us to Follow His Example of Lowliness and Costly Love

38. To Create a Band of Crucified Followers

39. To Free Us from Bondage to the Fear of Death

40. So That We Would Be with Him Immediately After Death

41. To Secure Our Resurrection from the Dead

42. To Disarm the Rulers and Authorities

43. To Unleash the Power of God in the Gospel

44. To Destroy the Hostility Between Races

45. To Ransom People from Every Tribe and Language and People and Nation

46. To Gather All His Sheep from Around the World

47. To Rescue Us from Final Judgment

48. To Gain His Joy and Ours

49. So That He Would Be Crowned with Glory and Honor

50. To Show That the Worst Evil Is Meant by God for Good

At the heart of Jesus's sacrifice is the work of God who put His own Son to death in order to pay the price for man's sin.

A 20th century cultural writer once attributed societal shifts in the 20th century to the loss of transcendence. He writes,

As a mass, 20th century humanity believes only in the present century, in the here and now, and nothing beyond it. Consequently, the dimensions of the beyond are reduced, that is, of eternal transcendence, and God in his creative and authoritative totality. The gospel speaks of 'the heavenly kingdom.' Man has become man's only goal, life the only goal of life, and time the only goal of time (DeRougemont 12).

The writer delineates three areas in society that influence man. They are philosophy, politics and church. Continuing into the 21st century, new standards, new values and new "normals" are established in society. If a new meaning or omission of sacrifice is set, the consequences are huge. The ramifications of which negates the sacrifice of Jesus.

An aspect of community is communion, not only by way of fellowship but also as the remembrance of the sacrifice of Jesus. Communion is the coming together unified under the Lord. By the sacrifice of Jesus, "there is one bread, we who are many are one body, for we all partake of the one bread" (1 Corinthians 10:17). Remembrance leads to thanksgiving and with a heart of full of gratitude we offer our bodies as tokens of thanksgiving, a living sacrifice for the Lord as He desires (Romans 12:1). Our bodies become as spiritual sacrifices onto the Lord (Stott). As spiritual sacrifices, the community of believers offer God honor, worship and praises. Prayer and humbleness of heart filled with faith waiting for the Lord as we endeavor to spread the gospel (Stott). The omission or lukewarm reception of sacrifice clearly demonstrates a disconnection with the transcendent meaning of the word.

Grateful and Forgive

The fact that one participant was able to associate a word for grateful but was unable to rate it is indicative of confusion. The magnitude of the consequences for the omission or redefinition of truth, sacrifice and the confusion regarding grateful in light of Jesus is becoming more evident. Forgiveness is one of the characteristics that defines the Lord but is barely understood by the participants. Half of the participants highly rated the word forgive, associating it with the words like trust, forget, love, friendly, friends and me. One quarter of the participants ranked the word forgive with little or no feeling. Their words associated with forgive were forget, friends and make-up. The rest of the participants gave the word forgive, a moderate feeling rating with forget and peace as their respondent words. One participant was silent with no response.

Ultimately, forget and friends were the prevailing associated words with one refusal. The common saying, "forgive and forget" although not true, may be the source of the predominate associated word, forget. Man can forgive but he cannot forget. Only God can forgive and forget by the blood of Jesus. Albeit, the command of the Lord is to forgive. Peter once asked Jesus, "'Lord, how often will my brother sin against me, and I forgive him? As many as seven times seven?' Jesus said to him, 'I do not say seven times, but seventy times seven'" (Matthew 18:21-22). "For if you forgive others, their trespasses, your heavenly Father will forgive you" (Matthew 6:14).

The frequent use of the word friends reflect a communal mindset, an insular or tribal (to use the vernacular trendy word) perspective that does not go beyond consideration of the individual. This may be due at least in part to the disconnection the Mosaics feel with the true community, the Christian church. They choose friends over faith (Kinnaman). The internet and a plethora of technological communication gadgets have influenced the Mosaic generation as no other. As a result their "reality is facilitating new patterns of learning, relating, and influencing the world, as well as changing the way they think about the church and Christianity.

Technological access allows them to experience and examine content originating from non-biblical worldviews, giving them ample reasons to the nature of truth" (Kinnaman 42). Therefore, has the meaning of the word forgive, which should have a singular one rooted in Jesus, been altered to fit a pluralistic worldview agenda? Has sin been so diminished that there is no sense of responsibility, thus no need for forgiveness. Data generated by the research certainly demonstrated the influence of media. This was confirmed in the use of associated words connected to the television daytime program, "Judge Judy," nighttime television series, "Pretty Little Liars" and the internet application "Angry Birds." Secular influence also prevails in Christianity where the spiritual essence of such words such as justice, law and rules are reinterpreted in a forensic sentiment (recall the New Testament scholar, N.T. Wright). Indeed, all questions raised thus far pose a need for further research.

Freedom

Another word in the Word Association Test that elicited concern is the word freedom. Five out of the twelve participants gave it a high rating, 4/12 a moderate rating and 2/12 had little or no feeling with it. The top associated words for freedom were American and flag. The words noted are symbols of freedom just as law was associated with the symbol of court. Could the sentiment be captured by the following statement? '"Freedom does not mean to *do what you want* but *to want what is called for*. I do not mean dictated by an outer authority but called for by an inner authority for the conscience which is responsive to what…is called 'the meaning of the moment'" (Sartre in Gould 147). Compare this statement with todays' notion rooted in critical theory,

> It is no longer the social atomism of neo-liberal individual individualism because it is not founded upon the self-determining Cartesian subject who asserts a choice by his or her will. Neither is it the Cartesian subject divided between a corporeal and an intellectual existence. The subject is situated and determined by that situation, it is the anonymity of Being – the way things are – which forces the subject to understand its finitude (Ward 113).

Both philosophies deconstruct the God given concept of freedom and rebuilt it to tie it with whatever. The following is an example of a deconstruction of freedom and woven into community.

> Community is no longer a substantive; it does not have a here or there, a specific location on a map with its boundaries drawn and outsiders

positioned... It is not based upon territory or exclusion. It is not a community contracted into. It exists before all contracts; it exists to resist all such exclusive, self – legitimating communities. It is radically heterogeneous and inclusive. In this is freedom... freedom is the community's exposure to time (Ward 107).

Freedom is a concept that is tantamount in the New Testament. It is the foundation of Jesus' work "for freedom Christ has set us free, stand firm therefore, and do not submit again to the yoke of slavery" (Galatians 5:1). "Let it be known to you therefore, brothers, that through this man forgiveness of sins is proclaimed to you and by him everyone who believes is freed from everything from which you could not be freed by the law of Moses" (Acts 13: 38-39). "But now that you have been set free from sin and have become slaves to God, the fruit you get leads to sanctification and its end, eternal life" (Romans 6:22). "Now the Lord is the Spirit, and where the Spirit of the Lord is, there is freedom" (2 Corinthians 3:17).

Acts 13:38-39 embodies all the words that captures the essence of the gospel. It also contains the words that were not recognized by the research group.

"Let it be known"---------truth

"through this man"-------sacrifice

"forgiveness"-------------forgive

"freed"---------------------freedom

If Acts 13:38-39 was read to a group of Mosaics, would they understand it? Based on the research data they would have difficulty with key words of the gospel. The gospel message that is contained within the verse is not appreciated by the Mosaic generation. They are lost.

It was determined that love is the foundation of the core process. Figure 2. depicts love based on the words noted by the participants in the research study. To explain love as presented by the research participants, the tool of deconstruction will be used. (If it is good for the goose, it is good for the gander.) There are basically two types of love, agape and eros, a polemic of love. Agape love is the Greek word for love and which the New Testament refers to. Eros is a love that is focused on the self and which seeks pleasure and self-gratification.

Agape love is a love that is distinctly Christian. Unlike eros love, agape love is a selfless one that is dedicated to the wellbeing of others and not motivated by self - interest. Agape love demands to love enemies as well. Dr. Dietrich Bonhoeffer explains it this way,

When we love those who love us, our brethren, our nation, our friends, yes, and even our own congregation, we are no better than the heathen and the publicans. Such love is ordinary and natural, and not distinctively Christian. We can love kith and kin, our fellow – countrymen and our friends, whether we are Christians or not, and there is no need for Jesus to teach us that. But he takes that kind of love for granted, and in contrast asserts that we must love our enemies. Thus he shows us what *he* means by love, and the attitude we must display towards it (*Cost of Discipleship* 136).

The model for the demonstration of the unique love that should characterize the Christian is found in one place and that is the cross of Christ (Bonhoeffer, Stott).

Using Hegelian dialectical thinking, (Osso, *Superficial Society*) agape love and eros love would be each other's opposite. Dialectical thinking dictates that there should be a synthesis or compromise between the two poles. The synthesis of the two could explain what love has become to mean for the Mosaic generation (see Figure 2). If the diagram in Figure 2 was flipped, it would reveal; Jesus through His compassion and sacrifice (LOVE) Happiness Joy Fellowship Family (Christian relationships and community).

The inverse logic that is evident is not new. It is a result of critical thinking that is taught in schools where one must consider all options and deny any authoritative stances (Osso, *Synthesis*). Hence, the ability to hold onto various perspectives. An example is the "'me – and –we – contradiction'. To generalize, they [Mosaics] are extraordinarily relational and, at the same time, remarkably self – centered…They want to do everything with friends and they want to accomplish great things under their own steam" (Kinnaman 29).

At this point, one can start to get a firm grasp of the core process.

Who I am is defined by an experience of spirituality as well as knowledge by belonging to a community, a social event that allows relationships and being true to oneself, both of which explain the how and what. My identity is tied to family as well as friends. I seek a big brother and respect the liberal/law alike.

The dualism found in today's thinking is one that tries to hold onto Christ and to culture as well, hoping for a synthesis of both. The battle lines for this exist in the heart and minds of man. On one side there is the flesh (self), eros, sin, the left hemisphere of the brain (secular culture) and the other is God (the Absolute and Good), the right side of the brain. Paul uses the same dualism in his letters to show how this dichotomy is reconciled in Jesus through His life, death and resurrection. There is no synthesis. But the evil one who is temporarily ruling the world till Jesus' second coming keeps the clash and deception alive.

Summary and Recommendations

The findings of the research using a Word Association Test demonstrate that there is a change within the English language that is causing a disconnection between the current generation and the preceding one. Philosophical and scientific arguments were presented in order to establish a foundation to the claim set forth. The questions that arose after data analysis attest to further research and inquiry into this phenomenon.

Grounded theory methodology used in the research proves that scientific inquiry can be employed to explore theological concerns. Therefore, more sociological research needs to be done in order to minister to the unsaved.

Language within language is one theory that has been substantiated with a small research sample. Further testing and intervention modalities by the Christian theological community is highly recommended to counter the atheistic stance of science. Technological advances have opened Pandora's box of information which is used to support their assertions. The recent Barna research of the Mosaic generation confirms the effects of media in the current technological age. No longer are the teachings from the Bible taken at face value, but are questioned. Critical theory and Hegelian dialectic are cited as influencing thought processes of this generation.

In the letter of Jude, the last letter before the book of Revelation, a warning is found about "certain people [who] have crept unnoticed who long ago were designated for this condemnation, ungodly people, who pervert the grace of God into sensuality and deny our only Master, Jesus Christ" (4). In the last days, there will be many of these deceptive people and Christians must contend harder for the faith. As Christians struggle to maintain the faith, they must also have "mercy on those who doubt, save others by snatching them out of fire; to others show mercy with fear, hating even the garment stained by flesh" (22-23).

Therefore, know the enemy in the various ways he manifests himself. Use what God provides and harness science to prove the Word of the Lord to those who say, "Wait, you lost me."

VII. SPEAKING TRUTH

In the devotional book by Sarah Young entitled, *Jesus Calling*, she writes as if Jesus is speaking. All the entries are based on Scripture which she notes at the end of the daily entry. The entry for January 28 states, "When My Presence is the focal point of your consciousness, all the pieces of your life fall into place. As you gaze at Me through the eyes of your heart, you can see the world around you from my perspective. The fact that *I am with you* makes every moment of your life meaningful" (29).

Indeed, keeping Jesus as the focal point of one's consciousness helps to interpret reality objectively and truthfully. As reality is internalized, the resultant thoughts, words and actions reflect the consciousness of the Lord. In John 14:6, Jesus is telling Thomas, "I am the truth." In Acts 17:24-26, Paul teaches the Athenians that God is the one and only God, the Absolute. He describes God as the One,

> who made the world and everything in it, being in it and being the Lord of heaven and earth. He does not live in temples made by man nor is He served by human hands as though he needed everything. And he made from one man every nation of mankind to live on all the face of the earth having determined allotted periods, that they should seek God, the hope that they might fall their way toward him and find him. Yet he is actually not far from each one of us. In him we live and move and have our being.

In order to understand truth we must understand God as the Absolute God. Within Acts 17:24-26, God is described as the Divine Creator whom the twenty-four elders and four living creatures in His throne room worship declaring, "Worthy are you, Lord and God, to receive glory, honor and power, for you created all things, and by your will they existed and were created" (Revelation 4:11). God is the Almighty Self Sufficient who does not require anything. He makes that clear in Isaiah 50:8-11 which states, "I will not accept a bull from your house or goats from your folds. For every beast of the forest is mine, the cattle on a thousand hills. I know all the birds of the hills, and all that moves in the field is mine."

Man is created in the image of God (Genesis 1:27). He did not create man like Himself, a god. The Hebrew word for image is "tselem" which means something that resembles another. The word is frequently used to connote a representative figure of another. Contrast the Hebrew word for image with the Hebrew word of likeness, "demut". Likeness in Hebrew refers to similarity in objects and is used when the focus is on similarity as opposed to the substance of a figure or depiction (Grudem). The image of God expression therefore, refers to "man resembl[ing] God, such as in the character of reason, morality, language, a capacity for relationships governed by love and commitment, and creativity" (ESV Bible 51). Compare the passage to Genesis 5:3 where it states that Adam fathered a son in his own likeness, after his image and named him Seth. Likeness demonstrates Seth's resemblance to Adam. "It is evident that *every* way in which Seth was like Adam would be a part of his likeness to Adam and thus part of his being 'in the image' of Adam. Similarly, *every* way in which man is like God is part of his being in the image and likeness of God" (Grudem 444).

God is Infinite, man is finite. Man is therefore, dependent on the Infinite God. Ephesians 1:11 states, "In him we have obtained an inheritance, having been pre-destined according to the purpose of him who works all things according to the counsel of his will. Because man is dependent on God, in him, we live and move and have our being." After all that is said and done, it can be confidently surmised that the source of all being is found in God.

Speaking truth requires the comprehension of three principles. They are; 1). God as Creator Who gives man his consciousness, 2). God is at the center of reality, and 3). The Bible as the written word of God is Truth. The interplay of the three principles shape human speech to reflect God's speech by providing structure and meaning. "Meaning is objective and absolute, not because a given linguistic expression of it but because there is an absolute Mind, God, who has communicated it to finite minds (human beings) through the common but analogous means of human language, which utilizes a transcendent principle of logic and being common to both God and humans" (Geisler and Roach 265).

God as Creator

God as Creator provides consciousness. When God created Adam and Eve, He provided for them all that was good (Genesis 2). God placed the two in the Garden of Eden, sometimes called paradise, with one request. He said, "You may surely eat of every tree of the garden, but of the tree of the knowledge of good and evil you shall not eat, for in the day that eat of it you will surely die" (Genesis 2:16-17). When Adam and Eve disobeyed the Lord and ate from the tree of knowledge of good and evil, a break took place. Having originated from God, the source of goodness,

Adam and Eve were now separated from Him. Formally their consciousness was for good, now it included evil. Adam and Eve were at once God's creation in His image yet at the same time against God. Where once upon a time humanity was the apple in God's eyes, humanity was later shunned by Him by their disobedience and losing all that was good (Genesis 3). To Adam He said,

Because you have listened to the voice of your wife and have eaten of the treeof which I commanded you 'You shall not eat of it' cursed is the ground because of you; in pain you shall eat of it all the days of your life; thorns and thistles it shall bring forth for you; and you shall eat the plants of the field. By the sweat of your face you shall not eat bread, till you return to the ground, for out of it you were taken; for you are dust, and to dust you shall return (Genesis 3:17-19).

Adam and Eve soon learned that this estrangement from God allows any and all evil to take hold of their consciousness. They experienced this in their two sons, Cain and Abel.

Abel was a keeper of sheep, and Cain as a worker of the ground. In the course of time, Cain brought to the Lord an offering of the fruit of the ground, and Abel also brought of the first born of his flock and of their fat portion. And the Lord had regard for Abel and his offering, but for Cain and his offering he had no regard. So Cain was very angry, and his face fell. The Lord said to Cain, 'Why are you angry, and why has your face fallen? If you do well [good] will you not be accepted? And if you do not do well, sin is crouching at the door. Its desire is for you, but you must rule over it' (Genesis 4:2-7).

Cain and Abel could very well represent the conscious, the knowledge of good and evil. Cain proved to be the evil one by murdering his brother (Genesis 4:8). The cold-hearted plan of Cain to accompany Abel to the field and then slay him demonstrates how calculating yet blinding an evil consciousness can become.

God's words to Cain, "if you do well [good], will you not be accepted? If you do not do well, sin is crouching at the door" was a reminder to Cain the consequences of focusing on self. When one focuses on self or anyplace other than God, the conscious "presupposes disunion with God and with man and marks only the disunion with himself of the man who is already disunited from the origin [God]" (Bonhoeffer, *Ethics* 28). Disunion with the Origin "means that the conscious is concerned not with man's relation to God and to other men but with man's relation to himself. But a relation of man to himself, in detachment from his relation to God and to other men, can arise only through man's self - deception of becoming like God. (28). Man's rebellion against God is the attempt to become equal to Him.

Everyone has a conscious but what sets the Christian apart? Jesus rectified it in the resurrection having defeated evil, and that rectory is fruitful in delivering people from the kingdom of Satan. The deliverance takes place at the beginning of Christian life, when we first believe the gospel. And the deliverance is also progressive, as we come to know the truth more deeply and cast off deception more thoroughly. The deliverance includes deliverance in thought, as our thinking moves from deceit to truth. It is also deliverance in language, because language and thought go together. We hear and speak truth in language. Receiving truth from Christ also helps us to be discerning; we become more adept at filtering it (Poythress 122).

There is a transformation of the mind or consciousness in Christ, whereby truth is discerned and spoken (Romans 12:2). By Christ, a reversal of consciousness takes place, one that takes the person back to the Creator, the Origin.

God as the Center of Reality

Dietrich Bonhoeffer was a theologian, scholar and a German Lutheran pastor who was imprisoned and eventually hanged by the Nazis in April, 1945. While in prison, Bonhoeffer was particularly known for his ability to remain calm even while other prisoners despaired as they watched others leave their cell, never to return. Bonhoeffer ministered to the prisoners by bringing to them the teaching of Jesus Christ. He modeled the character of Christ by his self- restraint and quietness during the most horrific times during World War Two (WWII). Nevertheless, there was conflict in him. While in prison Bonhoeffer wrote the following poem that describes the battle within him.

Who Am I?

Who am I? They often tell me.

I stepped from my cell's confinement

calmly, cheerfully, firmly,

like a Squire from his country house.

Who am I? They often tell me.

I used to speak to my warders

freely and friendly and clearly,

as though it were mine to command.

Who am I? They also tell me.

I bore the day of misfortune

equably, smilingly, proudly,

like one accustomed to win.

Am I then really that which other men tell of?

Or am I only what I myself know of myself?

Restless and longing and sick, like a bird in a cage,

struggling for breath, as though hands were compressing my throat,

yearning for colours, for flowers, for the voices of birds,

thirsting for words of kindness, for neighbourliness,

tossing in expectation of great events,

powerlessly trembling for friends at an infinite distance,

weary and empty at praying, at thinking, at making,

faint, and ready to say farewell to all.

Who am I? This or the Other?

Am I one person to-day and to-morrow another?

Am I both at once? A hypocrite before others,

and before myself a contemptible woebegone weakling?

Or is something within me still like a beaten army?

Fleeing in disorder from victory already achieved?

Who am I? They mock me, these lonely questions of mine.

Whoever I am, Thou knowest, O God, I am thine! (*The Cost of Discipleship* 15).

In the end, Bonhoeffer confidently says he is God's, that is, God being the center of his life and his reality. By focusing on the centrality of God in one's life, all that happens outside that focus will not influence the interpretation of reality and how to live life. Bonhoeffer knew that Christ had to be the center, not only for the individual but for the Church as well (Lutzer). World War II taught him as no academia could that this was essential in order for mankind to survive. Indeed, it is a matter of life and death. Bonhoeffer was appalled at how Nazi propaganda was able to supplant the message of the gospel by entering the German Christian churches (Lutzer). Holding onto God as the center of reality, Bonhoeffer was strengthened unto death. The last depiction of him comes from a description given by a doctor who was asked to witness his execution. He recorded,

> Between five and six o'clock, Bonhoeffer and three others were led to their execution. The doctor said that when the door opened, he saw Pastor Bonhoeffer still in prison clothes praying to the Lord, his God. The prisoners were ordered to strip. Then they were led down a flight of steps under the trees to a secluded area of their execution. Naked under the scaffold in the sweet spring woods,

Bonhoeffer knelt for the last time to pray. Then he climbed the steps to the gallows, brave and composed. Five minutes later, his life ended on April 9, 1945 (Lutzer 192).

Bonhoeffer was only 39 years old when he went to the Lord.

God as the center of reality happens when there is death to the old self and resurrection with the Lord (Galatians 2:2, Ephesians 2:6). Romans 6:1-14 explains death to the old self and sin. Verses 4-5 capsulate it as "We are buried therefore, with him by baptism into death, in order that, just as Christ was raised from the dead by the glory of the Father, we too might walk in newness of life. For, if we have been united with him in a death like his, we shall certainly be united with him in a resurrection like his." Death and life with Christ produces a mind of Christ in man (1 Corinthians 2:16). Just like Jesus focused His mind on the Heavenly Father, the mind of the regenerated man also does the same. When that happens, peace enters the mind of the person (Isaiah 26:3, John 14:22).

Therefore, in order to speak truth, the Lord must be the center of reality. What is observed with the senses is then interpreted with the mind of Christ. Thus, the perceptions are likened to the Lord. The Lord placed in the center of reality enables one to "destroy arguments and every lofty opinion raised against the knowledge of God, and take thought captive to obey Christ" (1 Corinthians 10:5).

The Bible as the Inerrant Word of God

Language in the Bible is primary to communicating the message of God. Attempts to debunk, alter and reason away the meaning of Scripture have a long history. Regardless, the language of Scripture have four characteristics that attest to its inerrancy. They are; God breathed, pure, perfect and true. "All Scripture is breathed out by God and profitable for teaching, for reproof, for correction, and for training in righteousness" (2 Timothy 3:16). Therefore, the Bible is the authority, the final say in matters that constitute righteousness.

Scripture is pure. "The words of the Lord are pure words, like silver refined in a furnace on the ground, purified seven times" (Psalm 12:6). The number seven is frequently used to mean completion, perfection and purity. Man can also maintain purity by "guarding it according to [His] word" (Psalm 119:9).

Perfection in the word of God is stated in Psalm 119:96 where the psalmist says, "I have seen the limit to all perfection, but your commandment is exceedingly broad." Whatever the Lord says or commands stems from His perfection. His words then, are truth. "Every word of God proves true; he is a shield to those who take refuge in him" (Proverbs 30:5). The veracity of Proverbs 30:5 was demonstrated in David's escape from his enemies and King Saul. In David's song of deliverance, he sings, "This God – his way is perfect; the word of the Lord proves true; he is a shield for all those who take refuge in him (2 Samuel 22:31). Indeed, "the sum of [His] word is truth and every one of [His] righteous rules endures forever" (Psalm 119:160).

Never changing, the Lord promised eternal life before the beginning of time (Titus 1:2). Scripture explicitly states, "God is not man, that he should be, or a son of man, that he should change his mind" (Numbers 23:19). He is the same yesterday, today and tomorrow (Hebrews 13:8). It is impossible for God to change because He is perfection and the "founder and perfecter of [the] faith" (Hebrew 6:18, 12:2).

The power of God's word written within the pages of the Bible has the ability to change peoples' lives. The Holy Spirit is the one who helps with the understanding of Scripture. These things God has revealed to us through the Spirit. For the Spirit searches everything even the depths of God. For who knows a person's thoughts except the spirit of the person, which is in him? So also no one comprehends the thoughts of God except the Spirit of God. Now we have received not the spirit of the world, but the Spirit who is from God, that we might understand the things freely given us by God (1 Corinthians 2:10-12).

The unsaved, "does not accept the things of the Spirit of God, for they are folly to him, and he is not able understand them because they are spiritually discerned" (1 Corinthians 2:14).

Jesus promised His disciples the illuminating capacity of the Holy Spirit after He ascended into heaven. In John 14:26, Jesus says, "But the Helper, the Holy Spirit, whom the Father will send in name, he will teach you all things and bring to your remembrance all that I have said to you." The disciples during Jesus' time did not have the New Testament with them because it was not written yet. They received the Holy Spirit as well as all future disciples of Christ as their Guide.

Later in the book of John, Jesus is quoted as saying to His disciples, "When the Spirit of truth comes, he will guide you into all the truth, for he will not speak on his own authority, but whatever he hears he will speak, and he will declare to you the things that are to come. He will glorify me, for he will take what is mine and declare it to you" (16:13-15). The promise of Jesus Christ continues today. Upon redemption, the Holy Spirit will dwell within and reveal God's will – the truth.

Speaking Truth is Learned

Reflecting on the data analysis of the presented research and the literature review, it can be stated with certainty that morals are relative. Postmodernism will lead to post- Christianity pushing beyond what little thresholds remain. These thresholds consists of "beginnings and endings, of birth, of death, or the sacred and the profane" (Ward ix). The postmodernists hope to cause discussions. To the committed believers, they are no different than Satan, the serpent saying, "Did God really say?" (Genesis 3:1). The experiment goes back to the 1960's with its countercultural push (Osso, *Superficial Society*). The hypothesis of the experiment is, a subject is taken out of the familiar and stable state of affairs and placed into a transitional space. In this way the subject is rendered 'naked' – that is, stripped of the roles and offices normative to life outside – and vulnerable. In this state, the impress of the other, the unfamiliar, can be felt and the subject challenged and transformed by the encounter (Ward x).

Viewing the present and the past generations in the light of this grand postmodern experiment, one can understand the disconnection between the generations. Speaking truth would have to be learned. Bonhoeffer explains this in his book entitled *Ethics*. He writes,

'Telling the truth'... is not a matter of correct appreciation of real situations and of serious reflection upon them. The more complex the actual situations of a man's life, the more responsibility and the more difficult will be his task of 'telling the truth.' The child stands in only vital relationship, his relationship to his parents, and he therefore, still has nothing to consider and weigh up. The next environment in which he is placed, his school, already brings with it the first difficulty. From the educational point of view, it is, therefore, of the very greatest importance that the parents in some way… should make their children understand the difference between these various circles in which they are to live and the difference in their responsibilities (359).

Bonhoeffer would know since he lived during the Nazi takeover of all societal institutions. Through Nazi propaganda, people were transformed into killing innocent people without any conscious regret. The Holocaust attests to that time in human history. To that effect, Bonhoeffer outlines three areas to know or be taught when speaking truth. Above all, Bonhoeffer states that, "God's truth judges created things out of love, and Satan's truth judges them out of envy and hatred. God's truth has become flesh in the world and is alive in the real, but Satan's truth is the death of all reality" (361). Choosing words is imperative. "Death and life are the power of the tongue" (Proverbs 18:2).

The following three areas are required when speaking truth. First, be aware of the relation between speaker and hearer. Speaking truth needs to take into consideration who is being spoken to, who is posing questions and what is the subject matter. The truthful words spoken essentially contain life and they need to connect with the other. If careful consideration is not practiced, the words may have the illusion of truth but lack the essence (spirit).

Second, be aware of the contexts, the content and boundaries. Be mindful of the fluidity of meaning between people and contexts. Recall the data analysis of the current research study, the frail meaning of freedom and the almost unrecognizable words, sacrifice and forgiveness. One can be speaking about freedom from a true sense rooted in the Lord, but the hearer does not comprehend. The word freedom does not carry any significance to the hearer. "When words become rootless and homeless, then the word loses truth and then indeed, there must almost inevitably be lying. When the various orders of life no longer respect one another, words become untrue" (Bonhoeffer, *Ethics* 362). The contradictory associated words noted in the Word Association Test confirm this.

Third, relate the object of the speech to the context in order to make an assertion. This requires a two fold approach involving discernment and timing. Discernment involves ascertaining what is at hand while considering the proper timing. Although, timing is always at the discretion of the Lord. To know His timing requires that each thought to be captive of Him (1 Corinthians 10:5).

Fourth, another aspect to learning to speak truth is knowing what is significant versus what is relevant. In a postmodern society, significance is not so much touted as is relevance. Sean Cort, author of *The Power of Perspective* writes, "The definition for significance and relevance is basically the same except for the defining feature for relevance and that is relevance connotes application" (120). Cort also notes that "God holds the key to always being significant and relevant at the same time" (121). For the postmodernist, significance and relevance is not in the hands of God but in their determination. The thought process is prophesied in 2 Timothy 3:1-2 which states, "But understand this, that in the last days there will come times of difficulty. For people will be lovers of self." Love of self is a preoccupation with self-awareness, self-regard and self-actualization. Thus, significance and relevance are part of this self- absorption and determination. This could explain the participant's (of the current study) confusion with the word sacrifice.

The confusion exposed what is significant and what is relevant. Cort states that we "must understand that whatever is relevant is always significant but whatever is significant is not always relevant" to someone (130). The rating scale employed in the Word Association Test measured the relevance by rating the words. Indirectly at least, the scale could measure how apt the participant would enact the word in daily living by the value he/she placed on it. The choice of words associated with the words in the test demonstrated the significance each word had with the participants. Here, the meaning of the associated word to the participant can be assessed and their sense of reality determined when the Bible (the truth) is used as the standard. When speaking truth to the present generation, the advice Cort gives resonates. He writes, "Take heed of the spirit of the moment and their day. Stay spiritually sensitive and in tune to what they are feeling and undergoing, spiritually and emotionally so that you can accurately and carefully ward off attack while still nurturing the sensitive tapestry of your relationship" (130).

Hurdles and Hows

How to speak truth dictates that one must jump over a few hurdles. The hurdles are 1). Propositional truth versus communal truth, 2). Faith versus spirituality and 3). Revealing truth through the Holy Spirit versus hearer (reader) response. Once these hurdles are conquered, the "how" of speaking truth can proceed. In speaking truth, one must,

1). Think bilingual.

2). Become a mentor.

3). Develop partnerships.

4). Lastly and most importantly, the goal of speaking truth is to re-center Jesus. Doing so, will lay the foundation for salvation. Each of the areas will be explained.

A big hurdle found in today's society is propositional truth verses communal truth. When speaking from a propositional stance, one is asserting a position or fact, a truth. Such an assertion carries with it authority, a finitude, an absolute; all in disagreement with the postmodern paradigm of thinking. Postmodern thinking is based on subjective truth because truth is relative.

All that is known comes from a communal experience (recall figure 4). The postmodernist's "ideas are relative to the community and are true for them. Propositions, to them, are not essential and have no universal criteria for distinguishing truth from error. They cannot even affirm that biblical propositions assert truth about reality. They are culture bound to the community "(Richison 168). The hurdle posed is no different than what Moses experienced when he encountered the Lord. "Moses said to God, 'If I come to the people of Israel and say to them, 'The God of your fathers has sent me to you' and they ask me, 'What is his name?' what shall I say to them?' God said to Moses, 'I AM WHO I AM.' And he said, 'Say this to the people of Israel, 'I AM has sent me to you'" (Exodus 3:13-14).

The Israelites were like today's generation who rely in their customs and traditions to determine what is true. Moses knew that his experience with the Lord would seem foreign to the Israelites. Declaring a personal relationship with the Lord seems foreign in today's world as well. Nevertheless, the Lord instructed Moses to gather the elders of the nation of Israel and tell them that He appeared to Moses. Moses was to communicate the following, "I have observed you and what has been done in Egypt, and I promise that to bring you up out of the affliction of Egypt to the land of the Canaanites, the Hittites, the Amorites, the Perizzites, the Hivites, and the Jebusites, a land flowing with milk and honey" (Genesis 3:16-17). God did not come across overbearing, but loving, offering help for the Israelites who found themselves in an oppressive plight. He offered hope and a way out of their situation. Today, the approach is modeled in the believer making an observation in the life of an unbeliever that would hopefully lead to discussion in the truth. Cognizant of the hurdle, the believer will proceed with love and care.

The second hurdle is faith versus spirituality. The spirituality that interests the present age is spirituality of self. The perspective is at the stark opposite end of faith in the Lord (1 Peter 1:20-21). If there is no meaning in one's life, the focus turns inward toward self. The observable behavior to serve self is demonstrated in illicit sex, drugs, aberrant behavior including suicide and excesses. The book of Ecclesiastes by King Solomon states, "Besides being wise, the Preacher [King Solomon] also taught the people knowledge, weighing and studying and arranging many proverbs with great care. The Preacher sought to find words of delight and uprightly he wrote words of truth. The words of the wise are like goads, and like nails firmly fixed are the collected sayings; they were given by one Shepherd" (Ecclesiastes 12:9-11). King Solomon jumped over the hurdles by being careful to choose words that the listeners would enjoy hearing while maintaining veracity. These words, in turn, served to encourage and guide hearers down a path that would lead to renewed life.

The third hurdle is revealing truth versus a hearer (reader) response. An illustration of this hurdle and how to overcome it is given by John Piper in the book, *The Supremacy of Jesus Christ in a Postmodern World.* The truth claim is "God – the Father, the Son, and the Holy Spirit, this one God – is the only one who has no beginning, and therefore, everything else and everyone else is dependent on him for existence and or value, therefore, less valuable than God" (72). Imagine the listener/reader response to this truth. There would be a total negation of

God, the Supreme Being, who is eternal, has always existed and all is dependent on Him. This Christian God is superior to them? No way!

Piper says that to show the listener/reader that their inferiority to God is really a good thing. Present the following questions:

Would you want to watch a football game where all the players were no better than you? Or watch a movie where the actors could act no better than you and were no better looking than you? Or go to a museum to see pictures by painters who could paint no better than you? Why are we willing to be exposed to all these places as utterly inferior? How can we get so much joy out of watching people magnify their superiority over us? The biblical answer is that we were made by God to get our deepest joys not from being superior ourselves but by enjoying God's superiority. All these other experiences are parables. God's superiority is absolute in every way, which means our joy in it may be greater than we could ever imagine (73-74).

Jumping over the three hurdles in todays' society should lead to a journey that involves thinking bilingual, becoming a mentor but not in the conventional way, fostering partnerships and lastly, re-centering Jesus. The presented research demonstrated that words have different meanings for the Mosaic generation. At times, certain words such as truth have no meaning.

Consequently, in order to communicate with the present generation, we must think bilingual. But unlike the typical meaning of bilingual where it is inherent to learn another language in order to be considered bilingual, the term jumps to a new level. The new level of bilingualism is speaking the same words but understanding the new language within the language. Bilingual in the present age is the understanding that certain words familiar to the speaker are not always understood by the hearer. The challenge is uttering the words that connect with the hearer.

Becoming a mentor today needs to be flipped. Mentoring is usually an older or wiser person who takes a younger or inexperienced person(s) under their wings and shares their wisdom with them. Today's generation would not tolerate such a position because it would seem too authoritative, too domineering and imperialistic. Reverse mentoring is proposed (Kinneman). In reverse mentoring, have the younger generation debate the faith. The questions and stances presented are windows of opportunities to speak truth to them. Remember the hurdles and engage the young in a loving manner.

Kinneman presents six perceptions by both the older and the Mosaic generations that may influence the course of mentorship. They have been modified via the research findings. They are,

Perceptions	Godly Outcomes
1). Overprotection of ideas	1). Discernment of truth
2). Shallowness	2). Leave it behind and follow Jesus
	(Discipleship)
3).Anti-science	3). Encourage knowledge and use of spiritual gifts each is endowed
	(Stewardship)
4). Exclusion/Alienation	4). Embrace the other as Jesus would
5).Repressive/intolerant tolerance	5). Relational-God's law is freedom which unifies people under Christ
6).Doubting	6). Doing- throw off the yoke of doubt and seek the Lord

Kinneman also notes that within the Christian community, a departmentalization of the young and old exists. This is particularly evident in the various groups within the church community i.e. youth groups, adult mission trips, children groups, etc. Since there is more disconnect between the generations than ever before, partnership between the older generation and the young is more important than ever.

Through partnerships, a sense of camaraderie is fostered that will eventually blur those dividing lines. Mutual respect, love and concern for each other grows as each develops in spiritual maturity. A partnership is akin to Jesus and the church with the Lord as the head. With the proposed partnerships, the older generation is the head of the Mosaic generation. In this partnership, the head's responsibility would be;

- Share wisdom that comes from God "to bring to light for everyone what is the plan of the mystery hidden for ages in God who created all things" (Ephesians 3:9).
- Live the truth so that others know what it is like to walk in the footsteps of the Lord.
- Share your story how darkness was conquered, revealing Light and a whole new life.

- Challenge the younger generation to use their renewed life in creative ways to serve the community.

Lastly and most importantly, re-position Jesus to the center. Meaning and being flow from Him. The focus is no longer on the community, friends or science but on the Lord. He is the source of happiness, joy, love and eternal life. The great preacher, Charles Spurgeon once considered:

The center of gravity is the substitutionary death of Christ…The pinnacle truth of Scripture, he affirmed, is Christ's death for the sins of His people: 'The great doctrine, the greatest of all, is that, God seeing men to be lost by reason of their sin, hath taken that sin of theirs and laid it upon His only begotten Son, making Him to be sin for us, even Him who knew sin he that believeth in Christ Jesus is made just and righteous (Lawson 94-95).

Summary

Speaking truth in a world that believes truth is relative poses challenges. Language has shown to have changed dramatically. Speaking a foreign language has evolved to speaking a language within a language. Much research needs to be done by believers, not just by the scientists, to gain a better understanding of the particular language within a language.

The understandings, hurdles, hows and suggested means to communicate truth that are presented is a start. Further study and development is strongly encouraged. Why the urgency? The sole reason is because "the end of all things is at hand" (1 Peter 4:7). Jesus spoke these words, "The harvest is plentiful but the laborers are few" (Matthew 9:37). Over two thousand years later, these words continue to resonate.

Today, there is a whole new generation that needs to hear the Truth and the laborers need to speak their language. The laborers must first believe that God is the Almighty Creator of all things. We are made in His image, originally with His consciousness. The first parent's disobedience caused a break in the consciousness shared with God. But through Christ, man has the hope of restoring that consciousness whereby truth is once again spoken.

God as the center of reality must also be the focal point of all laborers for Christ. Through this center, the interpretation of realty and one's walk in life is determined. The Bible as the inerrant word of God is the guide or map that one uses to travel in the life on earth. The words that comprise Scripture are God breathed and are to be used also in the ministering to the lost (2 Timothy 3:16). The words are ultimately the truth. They need to be heard by all and taught. The seed of truth must be planted. Prayerfully, the Holy Spirit will do the rest of the work.

"Therefore, pray earnestly to the Lord of the harvest to send out laborers into his harvest" (Matthew 10:38).

CONCLUSION

The purpose of this book is to raise awareness that language exists within language. The focus is on Christianity and the church where once language was considered a gift of God. The short term and long term effects on society were also discussed. Philosophical, scientific and theological perspectives were presented.

From a philosophical viewpoint, language is a private affair that is predicated upon the individual. Science deems language as an organism evolving through evolution with a common grammar standard in all languages. Theology barely maintains that language is a gift of God Who is the originator/creator of language and whose meanings are based on and measured by His words. Even in Christianity secular tools such as deconstruction and contextualization used in hermeneutics are inadvertently (or not) employed thereby causing a diversion away from truth. The consequences of the action causes redefinition of words once considered sacrosanct in foundational theology.

A recent book written by David Kinnaman, head of the Barna Research Group spotlighted a growing disconnection between the present and previous generations. This was evidenced in the response of the present generation (Mosaic) to the usual way of ministering by the church.

Their feedback was, "Wait, I don't understand. You lost me." If the present generation does not understand the current language used in spreading the Gospel, then the meaning of the words have changed. There must be a language within the language that the present generation speaks. To clarify, add scientific weight and create a theory for further investigation about the thesis that language within language may exist, grounded theory methodology was employed. From a sample size of twelve representing the Mosaic generation, the following data collection and analysis was produced. A Word Association Test created by the researcher was used to generate data.

Five top words caused confusion or were not recognized by the participants. The words were truth, freedom, forgive, grateful and sacrifice. The implications of the results and the gravity of the ramifications were not apparent until they were measured against God's words especially those found in Acts 13:38-39. It states, "Let it be known to you therefore, brothers, that through this man forgiveness of sins is proclaimed to you and by him everyone who believes is freed from everything from which you could not be freed by the law of Moses."

The message in the verse contains all the key words that the research participants had trouble with. "Let it be known" correlates to knowledge that is certainly true since the words of God represent truth. "Through this man" is a reminder of Jesus' sacrifice which is based on forgiveness. The purpose of the sacrifice is to free mankind from the bondage of sin, darkness and death. If mankind cannot understand the verses, then it is doomed to hell!

The urgency to counteract what is taking place is without having to say, of upmost importance. Some ways to oppose the incomprehension of Scripture were presented but here too, more research needs to be done in order to test their efficacy. (Scientific methodology, as was shown, can be harnessed and used for the glory of God.) The steps outlined are:

1. Think bilingual.
2. Become a mentor.
3. Develop partnerships.
4. Most importantly and to the end, re-center Jesus.

Bilingualism needs to be elevated from its customary meaning to a higher level in order to include learning the language within the language. In order to reach the present and future generations, the redefined words must be learned. Words that seem to be non-existent such as sin and hell are to be retaught like teaching a new language.

The roles in mentorship are reversed in order to fit in a reverse logic prevalent in today's society. By all means this does not imply compromise, subjugation or any type of yielding the truth. The mentor must exercise what Paul described in 1 Corinthians 9:19-23. Paul was willing to do whatever it took in order to gain entry into the lives of the lost. But he did not lose sight of the Lord. He maintained himself as a His disciple. Thus, mentoring allows the person being mentored to question while listening, learning and looking for doors of opportunities to minister by the mentor.

Develop partnerships within the church as well as in all structures of society. This includes political, social, economic and educational partnerships. If any impact against the tide of word redefinition is to be made, then the church must extend herself into all aspects of society. Her job is to re-center Jesus in society. Demonstrated in Figure

2, today love is defined by sex, joy, friend, family and God, sacrifice and compassion as the farthest from the definition. Flipping this paradigm of thinking puts Jesus at the top as the epitome of love re-establishing Him as the center of all being (sex, joy, friends and family).

Re-establishing Jesus as the center of all being provides the truth that is necessary to perceive reality as it truly exists. Since truth is relative in the current postmodern society, how is one able to discern truth? The answer is that they cannot because there isn't any. If there is no truth, then Jesus is reduced to simply a wonderful model for wholesome living. He will be relegated to the ranks of Buddha, Mohammed, Mother Earth and to the thousands of Hindu gods. All are considered equal to lead one to utopia, whether here on earth or in the spiritual world.

Language is integral in conveying the words of God. Christianity grew through language because "faith comes from hearing and hearing through the word of Christ" (Romans 10:17). Scripture warns that "on the day of judgment people will give account for every careless word they speak, for by [their] words [they] will be justified, and by [their] words [they] will be condemned" (Matthew 12:36-37). In the end, judgment will hinge on the words one speaks. Language can save or can cause death. To avoid death Paul writes in 2 Timothy 2:13-14, "Follow the pattern of the sound words that you have heard from me, in the faith and love that are in Christ Jesus.

By the Holy Spirit who dwells within us, guard the good deposit entrusted to you." "Follow the pattern of sound words" means to heed the meaning of sound words. Examples of sound words are truth, freedom, sacrifice, forgive and grateful. No clearer directive can be made. Language within language expresses not our mind but the mind, will and tongue of God. Therefore, the hope is that the questions generated as a result of the research data analysis will spur more study for the glory of God.

Universal Grammar (UG) which science touts and tries to confirm is an attempt to prove the theory of evolution. It is no more than a mirror version of God's language which rests on absolute truth. Man's struggle to match God by substituting God's words with man's redefined words continues in order to "make a name for themselves" (Genesis 11). The erroneous thinking is, of course, promulgated by Satan. It rages in the battlefield of the mind. "In their case the god of this world has blinded the minds of the unbelievers, to keep them from seeing the light of the gospel of the glory of Christ, who is the image of God.

For what we proclaim is not ourselves, but Jesus Christ as Lord, with ourselves as …servants, for Jesus' sake" (2 Corinthians 4: 4-5). Those who are not "conformed to this world, but [are] transformed by the renewal of [their] mind" speak using God's Grammar (Romans 12:2). Language and thought go hand in hand.

Whatever man's plans are, be it UG or any other theory to debunk God, will never go to fruition. When man speaks God's language, he is honoring God the Father, God the Son and God the Holy Spirit. The speech reflects God the Father as the source of meaning of the words. He "created all things and by [His] will they were created and were created" (Revelation 4:11). "In the beginning was the Word, and the Word was with God, and the Word was God. He was in the beginning with God. All things were made through him and with him was not any thing that was made" (John 1:1-3).

In creation, being (meaning) finds its foundation. The foundational meaning is firm, true and pure. And for the lovers of Christ, "He[she] must hold firm to the trustworthy in "sound speech that cannot be condemned, so that an opponent may be put to shame, having nothing evil to say..." (Titus 2:8). It seems that there has been no greater time than now to hold onto the true meaning in language. "Contend for the faith that was once for all delivered to the saints. For certain people have crept in unnoticed who long ago were designated for this condemnation, ungodly people, who pervert the grace of our God into sensuality and deny our Master and Lord, Jesus Christ" (Jude 3-4).

God's language and the language believers use (faith language) reflect God the Son as Unity. Indeed, mankind will be united under "one Lord, one faith, one baptism" (Ephesians 4:5). Therefore, it makes sense that Satan would want to mess the mind with confusion. Confusion causes disruption, division and discord. Confusion will lead to doubt about the deity and person of Jesus Christ which certainly "pervert[s] the grace of our God into sensuality and [denial] of our Master as Lord" (Jude 4).

The Christian nation is at high risk because the language spoken is not in unison. The plethora of Christian church denominations vying for congregants and claiming that they alone speak truth attest to a state of confusion, division and discord. They forget that Jesus is the Unifier. The indwelling Holy Spirit reveals the will of God and provides the extra special relationship with the Lord. "Those who live according to the Spirit set their minds on the things of the Spirit' (Romans 8:6). The mind "set on the things of the Spirit" speak God's language. Jesus said, "Therefore, I tell you, every sin and blasphemy will be forgiven, but the blasphemy against the Spirit will not be forgiven. And whoever speaks a word against the Son of Man will be forgiven, but whoever speaks against the Holy Spirit will not be forgiven, either in this age or in the age to come" (Matthew 12: 31-32). The pronouncement and warning by Jesus is tremendous in light of what is happening with language. "For if [man] live[s] according to the flesh [man] will die, but if by the Spirit you are put to death the deeds of the body, [man] will live. For all who are led by the Spirit of God are sons of God" (Romans 8:13-14).

Living a life by listening to the Holy Spirit is done by understanding God's language. If the Holy Spirit is cut off in any way to man, man is doomed to death. The life giving and life sustaining language of God that the Holy Spirit speaks to us is negated from reaching the lost. The intimate relationship between man and God is maintained through God speaking to man via the Holy Spirit and man praying to God using faith language, the God given gift of language. No wonder Jesus will not forgive anyone whose language blasphemes the Holy Spirit. "Faith comes from hearing, and hearing through the Word of Christ" (Romans 10:17).

The book of Mark records Jesus "proclaiming the gospel of God, and saying, 'The time is fulfilled, and the kingdom of God is at hand; repent and believe in the gospel" (1:14-15). The increasing ungodliness taking place across the globe confirm the urgency of Jesus' call to repent and believe. He began His public ministry with those words and believers are to do the same, speaking God's language to minister through fellowship, intercession and finally demonstrating a model for worship. Jesus tells His disciples as well as those proclaiming His words to, "Go therefore and make disciples of all nations, baptizing them in the name of the Father and of the Son and of the Holy Spirit, teaching them to observe all that I have commanded you. I am with you always, to the end of age" (Matthew 28:19-20).

The hope is that at the very least, the results of the research study conducted will cause Christians to think about how and what the new generation understands about the faith. The deep sense of urgency cannot not be more explicit especially in light of what Scripture says. One generation shall commend your works to another, and shall declare your mighty acts…They shall speak of the might of your awesome deeds…They shall speak of the glory of your kingdom and tell of your power, to make known to the children of man your mighty deeds" (Psalm 145:4, 6, 11-12). What God says will be done as is stated in these verses. Let His Word reach as many as people as possible across the world. Let His seed be planted in everyone's heart so that there will be a great awakening before the second coming of the Lord.

Do not say that what is happening with language is only a fad because in all fads, they come and go. "Do not say that there are yet four months, then comes the harvest? Look, I tell you, lift up your eyes, and see that the fields are white for harvest" (John 4: 35). "The great day of the Lord is near, near and hastening fast; the sound of the day of the Lord is bitter. (Zephaniah 2:14).

In the third letter of John, he writes about the early Christian church workers who traveled about in the name of Truth. He exhorts the believers to "support people like these, that we may be fellow workers for the truth" (8). God's Word is Truth (Colossians 1:6). And in the present world where there is no absolute, we need to be workers as the early Christians speaking His language while understanding the language within the language of the other.

APPENDIX

WORD ASSOCIATION TEST

1- strongly feel, 2- moderately feel, 3- little or no feeling

GENDER: M. or F.

WORD	RESPONSE	RATING
AGE		
love		
peace		
rest		
joy		
hate		
guilty		
compassion		
revenge		
freedom		
soul		
spirit		

heart

grateful

angry

forgive

WHAT IS THE FIRST WORD THAT COMES TO
MIND WHEN YOU READ THESE SENTENCES.

Love your enemies.

Judge not and you will not be judged

CIRCLE THE WORD THAT APPEALS TO YOU

spirituality or religion

faith or experience

knowledge or wisdom

individual or community

beliefs or belonging

belonging or identity

liberal or law

"where am I" or " who am I"

personal or social

how or what

relationship   or being true to oneself

family or friends

teacher or   friend

big brother or friend

WORD ASSOCIATION

1- strongly feel, 2- moderately feel, 3- little or no
feeling

WORD	RESPONSE	RATING 1, 2, 3
church		
law		
friend		
family		
knowledge		
religion		
truth		
God		
justice		
power		
enemy		
truth		

sacrifice

judge

reject

WRITE FOUR WORDS THAT DESCRIBE YOU

BIBLIOGRAPHY

Alberry, Sam. *Lifted. Experiencing the Resurrection Life.* Philipsburg, New Jersey: P and R Publishing, 2010.

Bartlotti, Leonard. "Seeing 'Inside' the Insider Movement: Exploring our Theological Lenses and Presuppositions," paper presented to the first Bridging the Divide Consultation, Houghton College, 23 June 2011, Houghton, New York.

Bible Dictionary and Concordance. New York, New York: Castle Books, 2009.

Bonhoeffer, Dietrich. *The Cost of Discipleship.* New York, New York: Macmillian Company, 1961.

_____ *Ethics.* New York, New York: Touchstone, 1995.

Brown, Colin, Peter Hagroot, eds. *The Neuro – Cognition of Language.* New York, New York: Oxford University Press, 1999.

Butler, Clark. *Hegel's Logic. Between Dialectic and History.* Evanston, Indiana: Northwestern University Press, 1996.

Carson, D.A. *Becoming Conversant with the Emerging Church.* Grand Rapids, Michigan: Zondervan, 2005.

Carter, Craig A. *Rethinking Christ and Culture: A Post – Christendom Perspective.* Grand Rapids, Michigan: Brazos Press, 2006.

Chomsky, Noam. *New Horizons in the Study of Language and Mind.* New York, New York: Cambridge University Press, 2007.

_____ "Language and Problems of Knowledge." *In The Philosophy of Language.* 5th ed. A. P.

Martinich, 675-693. New York, New York: Oxford University Press, 2008.

Christiansen, Morten and Nick Chater. "Language as Shaped by the Brain." 1 Jan. 2007. Santa Fe College. 1 Mar. 2014 <http://www.santafe.edu>.

Cobley, Paul and Litza Jansz. *Introducing Semiotics.* Cambridge, United Kingdom: Icon Books, 2007.

Collins, Francis. *The Language of God.* New York, New York: Free Press, 2006.

Corbin, John. "Code Writing Memos and Diagrams." In *From Practice to Grounded Theory,* eds.W.Carole Chenitz and Janice Swanson, 102-120. Menlo Park, California: Addison – Wesley, 1986.

Cort, Sean. *The Power of Perspective.* 2nd ed. Orlando, Florida: True Perspective Publishing House, 2012.

DeRougemont, Denis. *The Christian Opportunity.* New York, New York: Holt, Rinehart and Winston, 1963.

Driscoll, Mark. "The Church and the Supremacy of Christ in a Postmodern World." In *The Supremacy of Jesus Christ in a Postmodern World*, eds. John Piper and Justin Taylor, 125-147. Wheaton, Illinois: Crossway Books, 2007.

English Standard Study Bible. Wheaton, Illinois: Crossway Books, 2001.

Etymology Dictionary. 13 Jan. 2014 http://www.etymologyonline.com>.

Garner, David B. "High Stakes: Insider Movement Hermeneutics and the Gospel." *Themelios*, 37.2 (2012): 249-274.

Grudem, Wayne. *Systematic Theology*. Grand Rapids, Michigan: Zondervan Publishing House, 1994.

Geisler, Norman L. and William C. Roach. *Defending Inerrancy*. Grand Rapids, Michigan: Baker Books, 2011.

Gould, William B. *Frankel. Life with Meaning.* Pacific Grove, California: Brooks/Cole Publishing Company, 1993.

Hayford, Jack. *Living the Spirit Formed Life.* Ventura, California: Regal Books, 2001.

Hamilton, James. *God's Glory in Salvation Through Judgment. A Biblical Theology.* Wheaton, Illinois: Crossway Books, 2010.

Jackendoff, Ray. "The Representational Structures of the Language Faculty and Their Interactions." In *The Neuro – Cognition of Language,* eds. Brown, Colin, Peter Hagroot, 37-79. New York, New York: Oxford University Press, 1999.

Jennings, Nelson. "The Tapestry of Contextualization." In Mission to the World, comp. and ed., 24-30. *Looking Forward: Voices from Church Leaders on Our Global Mission.*

Enumclaw,Washington:WinpressPublishing, 2003.Johnson, Gary, Ronald Gleason, eds. *Reforming or Conforming? Post – Conservative*

Evangelicals and the Emerging Church. Wheaton, Illinois: Crossway Books, 2008.

Jones, Mark. *Antinomianism.* *Reformed Theology's Unwelcome Guest?* Philipsburg, New Jersey: P and R Publishing, 2013.

LaHaye, Tim. *Revelation Unveiled.* Grand Rapids, Michigan: Zondervan Publishing House, 1999.

Lewis, David. "Languages and Language." In *The Philosophy of Language.* 5th ed. A. P. Martinich, 656-674. New York, New York: Oxford University Press, 2008.

Lutzer, Erwin. *Hitler's Cross. How the Cross was Used to Promote the Nazi Agenda.* Chicago, Illinois: Moody Publishers, 2002.

Keller, Tim. "The Gospel and the Supremacy of Christ in a Postmodern World." *In The Supremacy of Jesus Christ in a Postmodern World,* eds. John Piper and Justin Taylor, 103-123. Wheaton, Illinois: Crossway Books, 2007.

Kinnaman, David. *You Lost Me: Why Young Christians Are Leaving Church...And Rethinking Faith.* Grand Rapids, Michigan: Baker Books, 2011.

Klein, William, L., Craig L. Blomberg and Robert L. Hubbard, Jr. *Introduction to Biblical Interpretation.* Nashville, Tennessee: Thomas Nelson Publishers, 2004.

Kripke, Saul. "On Rules and Private Language." In *The Philosophy of Language.* 5th ed. A. P. Martinich, 626-638. New York, New York: Oxford University Press, 2008.

Lawson, Steven J. *The Gospel Focus of Charles Spurgeon.* Orlando, Florida: Reformation Trust, 2012.

Locke, John. "Of Words." In *The Philosophy of Language.* 5th ed. A. P. Martinich, 621-625. New York, New York: Oxford Press, 2008.

Martinich, A. P. ed. *The Philosophy of Language.* 5th ed. New York, New York: Oxford University Press, 2008.

Metaxas, Eric. *Bonhoeffer. Pastor, Martyr, Prophet, Spy.* Nashville, Tennessee: Thomas Nelson, Inc., 2010.

Miller, Richard. *Surrender to the Spirit.* Shippensburg, Pennsylvania: Destiny Image Publishers, Inc. 2006.

Mounce, William, D. *Interlinear For the Pest of Us: The Reverse Interlinear for New Testament Word Studies.* Grand Rapids, Michigan: Zondervan, 2006.

Nee, Watchman. *The Breaking of the Outer Man and the Release of the Spirit.* Anaheim, California: Living Stream Ministry, 1997.

Osso, Maria." Knowing the Patient: A Process of Pattern Recognition." Master thesis. Florida Atlantic University, April 1995. Boca Raton, Florida.

_____.*Superficial Society.* 2nd ed. Orlando, Florida: True Perspective Publishing House, 2013.

_____.*Synthesis: How Hegelian Logic has Moved the Protestant Churches Towards a Christless Faith.* Orlando, Florida: True Perspective Publishing House, 2013.

Petchkovsky, Leon, Michael Petchkovsky, Philip Morris, Paul Dickson, Danielle Montgomery, Jonathan Dwyer and Patrick Burnett. "fMRI Responses to Jung's Word Association Test: Implications for Theory, Treatment and Research." *Journal of Analytical Psychology,* 58, no. 3 (2013): 409-431.

Piper, John. *Fifty Reasons Why Jesus Came to Die.* Wheaton, Illinois: Crossway, 2006.

Piper, John and Justin Taylor, eds. *The Supremacy of Jesus Christ in a Postmodern World.* Wheaton, Illinois: Crossway Books, 2007.

Poythress, Vern Sheridan. *In the Beginning Was the Word. Language. A God – Centered Approach.* Wheaton, Illinois: Crossway, 2009.

"Private Language Argument." 1 Apr 2014 http://www.dialecticonline.wordpress.com/issue-07-autumn10/the-private-language-argument/

Reformation 21. "Re: Insider Movements Defined...Biblically by Philip Mark." E-mail to Maria Osso. 12 June 2014.

Richards, Phillip Gary. *The Minister's Life of Obedience.* Orlando, Florida: Xulon Press, 2006.

Richison, Grant. *Certainty. A Place to Stand. Critique of the Emergent Church of Postevangelical.* Ontario, Canada: Castle Quay Books, 2010.

Roberson, Dave. *The Walk of the Spirit. The Walk of Power.* Tulsa, Oklahoma: Dave Roberson Ministries, 2012.

Rugg, Michael. "Functional Neuroimaging in Cognitive Neuroscience." In *The Neuroscience of Language*, eds., Colin Brown and Peter Hagroot, 15-36. New York, New York: Oxford University Press, 1999.

Shakespeare, Steven. *Derrida and Theology*. New York, New York: T and T Clark International,   2009.

Sim, Stuart and Borin Van Loon. *Introducing Critical Theory. A Graphic Guide*. London, United Kingdom: Totem Books, 2001.

Smith, James K. *Introducing Radical Orthodoxy: Mapping a Post – Secular Theology*. Grand Rapids, Michigan: Baker Academics, 2004.

Sproul, R. C. *The Consequences of Ideas. Understanding the Concepts that Shaped Our World*. Wheaton, Illinois: Crossway Books, 2000.

Stanford Encyclopedia of Philosophy. 19 Mar. 2014 < http://www.platostanford.edu>.

Stott, John. *The Cross of Christ*. Downers Grove, Illinois: IVP Books, 2006.

Tchividjian, Tullian. *Jesus + Nothing + Everything.* Wheaton, Illinois: Crossway, 2011.

Ward, Graham. *Theology and Contemporary Critical Theory.* New York, New York: St. Martin's Press, Inc., 2000.

Wells, David F. *The Courage to Be Protestants. Truth – Lovers, Marketeers and Emergents in the Postmodern Worlds.* Grand Rapids, Michigan: William B. Eerdmans Publishing Company, 2008.

Wright, N. T. *Justification. God's Plan and Paul's Vision.* Downers Grove, Illinois: IVP Academics, 2009.

_____*Pauline Perspectives. Essays on Paul, 1978-2013.* Minneapolis, Minnesota: Fortress Press, 2013.

Young, Sarah. *Jesus Calling.* Nashville, Tennessee: Thomas Nelson, Inc., 2004.

Zizek, Slavoz and John Millibank. *The Monstrosity of Christ. Paradox or Dialectic,* ed. Creston Davis. Cambridge, Massachusetts: Massachusetts Institute of Technology, 2009.

Scripture references marked ESV are taken from the *ESV Bible* (The Holy Bible, English Standard Version˚), copyright 2001 by Crossway, a publishing ministry of Good News Publishers. Used by permission. All rights reserved.

www.ingramcontent.com/pod-product-compliance
Lightning Source LLC
Chambersburg PA
CBHW031945080426
42735CB00007B/266